NORTH AMERICAN
OWLS

NORTH AMERICAN
OWLS

Journey Through A Shadowed World

Willow Creek Press

Published by Willow Creek Press, P.O. Box 147,
Minocqua, WI 54548

Editor/Design: Andrea Donner

Library of Congress Cataloging-in-Publication Data:

Burns, Jim, 1943-
    North american owls: journey through a shadowed world / by Jim Burns.
      p.cm.
    ISBN 1-57223-682-5 (hardcover : alk. paper)
 1. Owls--North America. I. Title.
QL696.S8 B86 2004
598.9'7'097--dc22

                                        2003025312

Printed in South Korea

This book is dedicated to my father,

Colonel James P. Burns, who left

for the Philippine theater of World War II ere

I saw the light of day, never to return.

His genes course deep within me.

To him I owe my great love for the natural world.

Though un-met, he has been my companion

every step along the way.

Contents

Introduction

THE IDEA FOR THIS BOOK WAS conceived when my wife and I returned from a trip to Churchill, Manitoba, in the summer of 1998 and discovered that I had, indeed, captured on slide film the image of a Northern Hawk Owl moments after it had ripped the leg from an Arctic Hare and was carrying that morsel to one of its three young that had recently left the nest. Knowing how extraordinarily privileged we were to have witnessed this once-in-a-lifetime insight into the mostly occluded realm of owls, I began casting about for some way to share it with others who love the natural world as much as I do.

When I mentioned the concept of the book to a birding friend, his reaction was "Does the world really need another owl book?" His well-taken point was that there are already many fine books about owls out there. Owls have fascinated man since the dawn of recorded history and, in the earlier years of that history, owls were all about myth and mystery. Most of the recent books

about owls have been about shattering that aura and reducing that myth and mystery — "scientific" books intent upon presenting owl facts and clarifying owl fiction. It is my intent to swing the pendulum back the other way! With familiarity comes trivialization. It is my hope that there is never anything trivial about this remarkable family of nighttime raptors, or the highly specialized niche they fill in the largely unseen and mostly unimaginable natural world they patrol.

Another friend, to whom I gave a few chapters before the book was finished, felt that I was equivocal in my presentation of owls and left readers with no conclusions about how they should feel about them. No kidding! I'm still feverishly working on my own conclusions even as you read these chapters. To me, the improbabilities of the natural history of owls and the seemingly inexplicable nature of much of their existence is what make them appealing, enthralling, and if you will, just plain fun. I *want* to perpetuate those ancient myths and propagate those unfathomable mysteries! They may not define owls for us, but they define who *we* are as a species.

For me, owls are a metaphor for the natural world and for life itself. Just like you, I'm seeking answers that I'm not at all sure I want to find. Answers I may not understand. Answers I may not want to understand. But I'm a lifer and I have to look. I would prefer not to see my owls laid out upon the professional ornithologist's dissecting table. I want my owls shrouded by shifting shadows under a gibbous moon. It is who I am. I think that is who we are as a species.

This book recounts my most memorable encounters with each of the nineteen North American owl species. Though I have included useful and interesting information on each, it will not tell you precisely how to look for them, exactly where to find them, or how to unfailingly identify them if you are fortunate enough to see one. This is not a guide books to the owls. This is a guide book to my soul. Maybe you have found yourself searching for something along some of these same traces. How do you view the natural world? How do you fit into that world? Can that world be preserved? Do you want it preserved? My apologies, but to me the questions are more important than the answers. That makes me a human being. And an unapologetic lover of owls.

May you spend many years seeking owls. And may a few find you along the way.

Glossary

bander: A person, either professional ornithologist or trained volunteer, who captures birds with mist nets, records their weight and general health, places a band with date and location on their leg, then releases them. Banding is a major source of our knowledge of birds' migratory status and population fluctuations.

birder: A person who actively seeks out birds to watch and study in their own environment: sanctuaries, specialized habitats, etc.

birdwatcher: A person who passively enjoys watching and studying birds which show up wherever he or she happens to be: backyard birdfeeder, office window, picnic in the park, etc.

brancher: The term used for a young owl, just out of the nest and as yet unable to fly, but strong enough to cling and climb around on the branches of the nest tree.

bumbles: Kids. A term used for the young of the human species under the age of ten, derived from the sense that their general activities are often rambling and free of focus or purpose.

Cooper: A Cooper's Hawk, an accipiter which hunts by day in forested areas and will take small and medium sized owls.

crepuscular: Active at dawn and dusk. Most bird species are active by day — diurnal. Some of our owl species are strictly nocturnal — active only by night in total darkness. Many owls are crepuscular.

eight-hooter: The vernacular name used by many birders for Barred Owl, derived from the eight distinct syllables in its most commonly heard call.

five-hooter: The vernacular name used by many birders for Great Horned Owl, derived from the five distinct syllables in its most commonly heard call.

headsets: The dark spotting on the head of female and young Snowy Owls, which distinguishes them from the mostly pure white older males, giving the appearance of the bird wearing earphones atop an otherwise white face.

lifelist: The record, kept by a lister, of the first time a species is seen. A birder may have seen hundreds of American Robins, but the very first one was his "Life" American Robin and is recorded on his lifelist.

lister: A birder who keeps a checklist of species seen.

mantle: A verb, the term used when a bird of prey, perceiving some intrusion or threat, covers its meal with wing or entire body as if to shield or protect it.

molt: A noun or verb, this term refers to the periodic feather replacement which birds undergo as plumage becomes worn through usage. Typically each species has its own regular timing and pattern of molt.

owling: Looking for owls.

primary: One of the longer, outermost flight feathers on a bird's wing. There are typically nine to twelve primaries depending on the species.

Questar: The "Cadillac" of spotting scopes, superior to all others in light gathering and resolution; sometimes called simply a "Q."

scapulars: The feathers at a bird's "shoulders," the area of the upper back where wings attach to the body.

SEOW: The bird banders' four letter shorthand for Short-eared Owl.

stoop: A verb, the term used for a bird of prey dropping, from the sky or from a hunting perch, onto a prospective meal.

taping: Playing a tape recorded call of an owl species for the purpose of luring the owl into view, typically after dark.

tick: A verb, this term refers to checking off a species on one's lifelist.

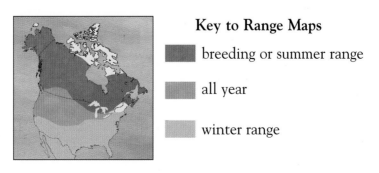

Key to Range Maps

breeding or summer range

all year

winter range

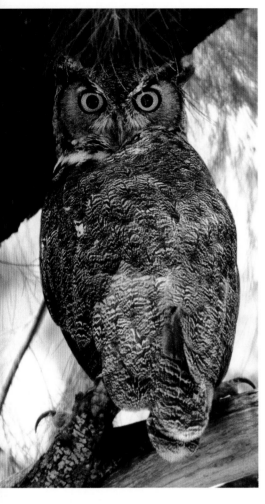

Chapter One
Great Horned Owl

The Great Horned Owl is our most widespread owl, with its low hoo hu-hu hoo hoo a familiar sound in much of North America. They are distinguished from other owls by their large size, widely-spaced ear tufts, white throat bib, and the dark cross-barring on their underparts. Their plumage varies from the pale gray of the Canadian tundra, to the dark, heavily marked birds of the wet Pacific coast forests (such as the one in the photo to the right).

A Talisman From the Emissary

IMAGINE FOUR PILGRIMS only just embarking on a lifelong journey for "The Grail," thinking "It" will appear momentarily, being only a lifetime short of realizing the journey *is* the grail. Imagine four skeptics huddled around a Thermos of hot chocolate in the middle of the night, in the middle of the winter, in the middle of Iowa. A wildlife biologist, the most recent incarnation in a lineage direct from Merlin to apothecary to shaman, has slipped them a tape. "Play this tape," she has cackled. "The owl will come."

Five-hooter. They have seen one once before, years ago and quite by chance. On a bitter winter's day, roosting in the tangles of a shelterbelt, perfectly camouflaged were it not for the illuminating shaft of sunlight falling directly upon it, size and protruding ear tufts leaving no doubt as to its identity, it had deigned to allow them close approach and silent study, the warmth of its private ray no doubt overriding its natural wariness.

The Great Horned Owl is a large, powerful, and mostly nocturnal owl. It has probably the most diverse habitat and climatic tolerance of any North American owl.

But to summon one to themselves? Surely this was madness. Still they persevered, added more marshmallows to the steaming potion in the cups, punched the rewind button one more time. The thermometer, hovering near single digits, chronicled a cold that had long since sucked the warmth from their toes and was now sucking energy from the batteries. It was a cloudy moonless night too cold to snow.

"Hoo hu-hu, hooo hoooo."

Five-hooter. Deep. Resonant. Seeming to emanate from the very bowels of the earth, the calls from the tape filled the black forest, filled the two adults with a primal awe, and filled the two little people with that delicious mixture of anticipation and apprehension that little people seem to thrive upon. Their little circle grew tighter around the flickering lantern.

Great Horned Owl

They recounted anew the scary stuff the literature had revealed. Great horned owls were big! The largest of the owls by weight, if not by size, they were as big as Red-tailed Hawks and they had been known to *take* Red-tails! Great Horneds were seemingly undeterred by all those animal defenses so deterring to man. They had been known to take *skunks*. They had been known to take *porcupines*. Snakes were a not-uncommon portion of their takings, as were smaller owls. They nested earlier than any other species to take advantage of the later nesters as food for their already-hatched young.

Imagine preschoolers hearing this litany by flickering lantern light in the dark woods while anticipating Five-hooter's imminent arrival. But the batteries were dead now, the hot chocolate down to the dregs. The priestess surely had misspoken. The potions were too weak. Or perhaps the owls, rewarding only those of unwavering faith, had sensed the pilgrims' skepticism.

Just as the word was given, just as the circle began to open, some faint stirring swept the clearing. Not a breath of wind this night, but frozen saplings tinkled together and a bough creaked softly.

"*Ho, hu-hu, hooo hoooo!*"

Four breaths caught and every hair on every scalp began to crawl. Every head whirled to the tape recorder, lying untouched, within the circle, the batteries cold and dead. *The batteries were dead!*

Unsteady hands groped for the searchlight, unused till now, its batteries still viable. The beam started up the huge bole, splaying left and right to scour the darkness from the horizontal limbs. "*Hoo hu-hu, hooo hoooo!*" It was there, thirty feet up, an apparition scarce to be believed, unblinking yellow eyes ablaze in the flashlight's glare — for just a moment. Then it was gone as it had come, into the darkness on silent wings.

Stricken, the four pilgrims could not breathe, were incapable of speech as they sorted through their jumbled emotions — elation that this seance had succeeded; regret that the encounter had been so brief; relief that the

Great Horned Owl
Bubo virginianus

Most frequently heard vocalization
5 syllables on one pitch, "Hooo, hoo-hoo-hooo, hoooo"; very deep and resonant; heard year-round, but especially during wintertime courtship.

Size
A large owl, about 18" long, with a wingspan exceeding 4 feet. They can weigh up to 5 pounds.

Most notable physical features
• large ear tufts (the "horns")
• mottled brown body with conspicuous white throat bib
• huge yellow eyes
• heavily barred beneath

Seasonal movement
Non-migratory; permanent resident

Nest sites
They typically use prior nests of large birds such as hawks and herons, or lay eggs in such places as barn lofts or cliff cavities. Nesting commences earlier than any other native bird, in January and February.

Habits
Nocturnal but often seen at dawn and dusk; occasionally found on daytime roost.

Range/habitat
Great Horneds range throughout North America, and can be found in forests, swamps, saguaro deserts, shelter belts and river bottoms.

Great Horned Owls commence nesting earlier than any other native bird, in January and February, so that nestlings are growing and fledge in April and May in synchrony with the emergence of the spring's first crop of young field mice and rabbits.

specter had vanished; chagrin that they had shown so little faith; uneasiness with the dawning awareness that this pilgrimage had really only just begun. Four novice birdwatchers forever hooked on owls and owling.

I T IS A BELIEF HELD BY SOME that the Great Horned Owl, at once the largest, most powerful, vocal, and ubiquitous of the owl family, has been sent by the other owls, an emissary as it were, to satiate our owl-need, so that the rest of the family, smaller, quieter, more retiring and unobtrusive, less cosmopolitan, can remain undisturbed along the peripheries of man's society and consciousness.

Great Horneds are at home from the treeline in the north to the Saguaros of the southwestern deserts, and to the cypress

Great Horned Owl

swamps of the east coast. They are heard more often than seen because of their deep, sonorous voice. They are seen more often than other owls because their great size renders them more conspicuous on daytime roosts. They will inhabit stands of timber within our eastern cities as well as vegetated washes within our western cities.

Great Horneds have been called hunting machines. They are not migratory as are some of the smaller owls, and neither are they winter irruptives. The most generalized feeders of our avian predators, they are at home in any habitat and at all seasons because there is always something they will eat. In short, though it seems at odds with their "owlness" to say so, Great Horned Owls are common.

Though I have long since stopped entering every record of the more common bird species in my field notes, ever since that Great Horned night in Iowa when we first "called up" an owl, I have

Rather than build nests, Great Horneds typically use prior nests of other large birds, such as hawks or herons.

never failed to record each and every owl sighting and owl "hearing." For several of the owl species I have less than a dozen records in a lifetime of birding. My records for Great Horneds run to the hundreds, and this without really ever looking for them, as we have for its less-common brethren.

In a summer spent working on the coast of South Carolina, Great Horneds were a yardbird. On a Christmas Count in a road-closing snowstorm in Arkansas, they were the first bird recorded for the day; on a Christmas Count in a road-closing snowstorm in southeastern Arizona, they were the last bird recorded for the day. We have seen Great Horneds perched on fence wires on Pt. Reyes in California. We have seen them

The plumage of the Great Horned Owl varies according to its location. Birds in the western interior are typically pale and grayish in tone, as seen below, while those in the eastern part of the continent are more richly colored. As in other owls, females are generally browner and more heavily marked than males, although this difference is often difficult to distinguish.

copulating at Picacho Reservoir in Arizona. We have found them nesting in a farmloft where we expected barn owls. We have found them nesting in saguaros where we expected elf owls.

We have not seen Great Horneds fishing, as some have reported, but we have seen them exhibiting what can only be a very opportunistic hunting technique: we have seen them sitting on paved backroads at night, hovering ("kiting") over the road, slapping their wings together — waiting for rodents attracted to the warmth of the road surface. They scare (or herd) these rodents from the road margins for an easy meal on the blacktop.

Great Horned Owl

We have had Great Horned Owls fly in to investigate a Ferruginous Pygmy-Owl tape, and fly in to investigate a Spotted Owl tape. In both cases we immediately ceased and desisted for fear our "prey" would become their prey.

The most unexpected place we have seen a Great Horned was the one teed-up, at dusk, on an iron bar imbedded in the slag pile of an abandoned mine, and the most prescient place we have seen one was the one that flew over the nightly ranger show at Mammoth in Yellowstone National Park. The talk that night was on owls of the park.

Great Horned Owls are sometimes commonly called Hoot Owls, Cat Owls, or Winged Tiger.

If there is ever a reason you need to satiate your owl-need right now, guaranteed, you should go to one of two places — any shelterbelt on any of the national wildlife refuges in the west, or any rural cemetery out a ways from any small town in the west — Great Horned Owl guaranteed.

ONCE IN THE FOOTHILLS of the Cascade Range in eastern Washington, we came across a dead Great Horned Owl. Not yet stiff, indeed still warm, it was far from any road and had no sign of external trauma. After a moment of silent hesitation, I hefted it, then passed it around for closer examination, the wingspan wider than the smallest member of our party was tall.

The hefting, the passage, the examination, all took two hands, hands that were holding a textbook on evolution. Evolution: *The gradual process in which something changes into a more complex form.* And how do you explain evolution to the smallest member of your party who is holding a dead bird of prey, nearly his size, with equal parts fear and wonder?

Great Horned Owls are often seen at dusk, perched on telephone poles, wires, fences, and trees.

Slowly and tactilely. We paged through the text, a text begun long before the evolution of our own species began — the huge eyes, nearly the size of our own; the facial discs to gather and concentrate nightsounds for the ears; the asymmetrical ear openings to triangulate the exact source of those nightsounds in total blackness; the serrations on the leading edge of the first primary to mute the sound of flight; the marvelously-curved and sharp talons to grasp and hold the prey.

Daylight and death allayed some of the fear. The intricate

Great Horned Owl

efficiencies evolution provided this perfect hunting machine increased the wonder. An hour passed in seeming minutes. No one spoke to leave. Where else was there to go? Where else to be when imponderable answers lie within the tightening circle of heads, answers to imponderable questions first realized on that wintry Iowa night where the pilgrimage had begun? Surely no sorcerer nor shaman, no schoolbook nor renowned lecturer, could ever compel such enthralled attention.

How do you take leave of the scene of a death that has become a textbook explication for the process of life? We took a vote. We had the one requisite vote for interment. We had one chivalric vote for an evening bonfire to the gods of owling. We had two votes (adult and so environmentally proper) for leaving the scene as we had found it. Then we had the great debate. And then the great debate needed to be ended with the requisite speeches regarding the chain-of-predation and the web-of-life.

The four pilgrims plucked a single, serrated primary, a talisman to insure them owl-speed, silent and swift, on the long and winding road.

Great Horned Owl wing from above and below.

Chapter Two
Barred Owl

Best detected by sound, Barred Owls deliver one of the most recognizable calls. The distinctive, clear-voiced rhythm of the hoots is often rendered as "Who cooks for you, who cooks for you all" (Hoo hoo ho-ho, hoo hoo ho-hooooaw). The descending and rolling "you all" (hooawww) is characteristic of the species. Barred owls can be heard during any night of the year, and occasionally during daylight as well. They will also emit wild-sounding yawls and chuckles, and a tremendous variety of barking, cackling, and other "crazy" sounds.

Crazy Owl

OWLS NEVER APPEAR *when and where they are expected.* This is the first rule of owling — Owling 101. It is a rule all initiates are taught on their first night. Arctic cold or tropic heat, bright moondance or murky fogsbreath, it makes no difference. That first time out, consciously seeking the unknowable, owls will not appear, will remain unknown. Initiates must pay their dues, must be teased, tantalized, and enticed. All nineteen species of North American owls know this, are clairvoyant, are in on this vast charade.

Owls always appear when and where they are least expected. This is the first corollary of owling — Owling 102. It is a corollary shown to the enlightened only after the requisite dues have been paid. This, owls also know. Typically, the unexpected appearance of any owl is accompanied by one of two things (often both): head-snapping, heart-pounding adrenaline, and/or loss of sleep.

The apparition of the emissary sent to our first owl seance

Male and female Barred Owls are identical in plumage.

deep in Iowa's winter (though of course we didn't realize it at the time), was totally a fluke of nature, an act of the birding gods, some contravention of all the known laws of owling. Either we were being blessed or we were being set up; with owls, one can never be sure. And after our introduction to the first corollary, Owling 102, we still weren't sure.

It began as most early owl episodes do, with the aspiring birders clueless and unsuspecting. On a springtime visit to relatives in northern Missouri we had gotten a later-than-anticipated start from our home in central Iowa. Rather than intrude on our hosts in the middle of the night, we decided to stay at a state park along our route. Pitching our tent well after dark with a practiced efficiency not often associated with a four-person party (including nine- and four-year-old males), we dove into our sleeping bags promising first thing in the morning to explore the natural history behind the name of the park — Nine Eagles.

Often in those fraught moments between awakening from sound sleep and being fully sentient, the dreamer tries to remain *in* a good dream… or hopes that what the slumbering senses are conveying is *only* a bad dream and tries to exit as quickly as possible. In a dark tent in the middle of a dark night, the former is much preferred. If the dream be scary enough, or the tent and the night black enough, where lies the preference in the latter case?

"Hoo, Hoo, Hu, Hoooo, Hoo, Hoo, Hu, Hooooaaw!"

Instantly I knew this was no dream. Neither dying banshees nor the Prince of Hell could have concocted this aural nightmare, at this many decibels, so close it seemed inside the tent with us. This went way beyond unnatural, and took me in a heartbeat from fearing the dream to fearing the awakening, and told me in an instant that three other pairs of eyes were surely bugging out, though not a word was spoken, not a breath released.

"Who Cooks For Youuuu? Who Cooks For Youuu Awl!"

There certainly being no way I was going to move a muscle or make a sound that might betray our presence to this unfathomable thing in our impenetrable dark midst, my mind released a silent scream and began careening through the possibilities, lurching from natural to surreal. Even here in Nine Eagles State Park, I knew these were no eagles. Nine hundred eagles could not approximate this demoniacal cacophony. And eagles are not creatures of the night.

Creatures of the night! Cougars? Not likely on Iowa farmland. Feral catfight? No, this was deep and resonant, not shrill. Visitation from my great aunt Mad Winnie, who had died estranged from the family? Come on, get a grip. Cattle bawling through fog settling on the river? Ever hear cattle bawling in cadenced phrases, exactly duplicated several times within a minute? Fellow campers in drunken revelry? Though we had seen no other tents in our area, my free-falling brain wishfully clung to this notion as the only viable one outside of the unthinkable, the unimaginable.

"Jim, are you awake? Do you hear the owls?"

Luckily for the three males in the tent, we had with us one pragmatic, well-grounded female to grab the family rudder in this latest of our frequent fantasy moments. Luckily she remembered what our wildlife biologist/owlmistress had warned us within the year — "The first time you hear a barred owl up close, you're not going to believe it."

Eight-hooter! Deep. Resonant. Maniacal. Seeming to emanate from the dark recesses of the tent itself, from the darkest closets of a denatured mind in fanciful flight to some planet on the other side of reason. Eight-hooter. If you sleep in its territory you will not sleep. By the time these cater-

Barred Owl
Strix varia

Most frequently heard vocalization
8 syllables, "Hooo hoo ho-ho, hoo hoo ho-hooaw"; rhythmic, expressive, and loud

Size
A large owl, 21" long with a 44" wingspan. They weigh about 1.5 lbs.

Most notable physical features
• Large, stocky with round, puffy head
• broad-winged and short-tailed
• large, moist brown eyes
• chest is barred; belly is streaked lengthwise
• white spots on back

Seasonal movement
Non-migratory; permanent resident

Nest sites
Natural tree cavities and abandoned stick nests of crows and squirrels; a pair may use the same nest site for many years in succession. As is typical of owls, young leave the nest at a few weeks of age, well before they can fly. The flightless owls are called "branchers." Their parents will continue to feed them for several more weeks, often until they are beyond 4 months of age.

Habits
Nocturnal; occasionally heard during the day or flushed from dense cover

Range/habitat
Barred owls range from the eastern U.S. across central Canada, and are colonizing south through the Pacific Northwest

wauling zombies of the Grand River hardwood swamps had finally desisted for the night, the sun was already a glow of promise beneath the horizon and fright had long since evolved through wonder and delight into grumpiness.

And they weren't through with us yet. After breakfast, still half bewildered, we searched the woods for two hours seeking some glimpse of the suspects, any concrete evidence to verify our midnight visitation. Not a trace. Exiting the park, we stopped a ranger for a reality check and to take the pulse of our doubting senses. Could we possibly have heard Barred Owls in the park last night? Where could we *see* one? He just chuckled and gave us the smile of the long-since initiated. We figured he *was* a Barred Owl in disguise, just part of the grand ruse.

THE BARRED OWL IS a large owl, widespread over much of the country east of the plains, but not quite as large as Great Horneds nor at home in as many habitat niches. It is not as aggressive, not as catholic in its choice of prey, not as vocal — and thus not as easy to find and observe as Great Horneds, despite its dismaying and certifiably insane vocal repertoire. Indeed, "Crazy Owl" seems to prefer denser woods and deeper swamps because these preclude competition and attack from "The Tiger Of The Night," the Great Horned Owl.

Understandably for a species that reaches its highest population densities in the murky, moss-enshrouded cypress swamps of the Southeast, Barreds have a long-standing and well-deserved reputation as skulkers. Though they can be quite responsive to imitations of their call at the beginning of the breeding season, typical encounters are of two types: the pilgrim will hear a Barred calling but will not be able to find it; a Barred will find the pilgrim without having called or revealed its presence in any way. A Barred will often foil the faithful, particularly at night, by coming in unseen, silently observing the observers until they leave, *then* responding with vocals. Which of course the now *non*-observers hear from up to a mile away as they retreat, cursing softly, through the stumbledark woods.

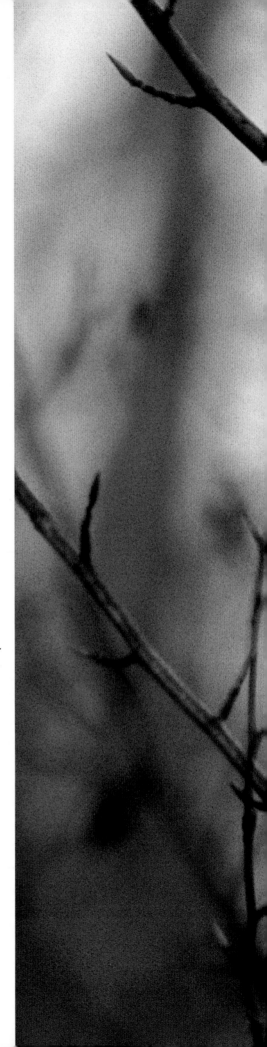

Barred Owls may be heard in the late afternoon and therefore, can be tracked down in the daylight. If found roosting during the day, they can be remarkably tame and observers can sometimes get quite close.

Ever the devious prankster, Crazy Owl has perfected this now-you-don't-see it/now-it's-there ploy on a much broader ecological and geographical front. Following river bottoms and ribbons of boggy ground and deep timber across the Canadian prairie provinces, Barred Owls have established thriving populations in the Canadian Rockies and begun colonizing up and down the Cascade Range in the Pacific Northwest. There have been sightings in Alaska, rumors in California, and documented interbreeding with the smaller, less aggressive, less cold- and heat-tolerant Spotted Owl in Washington and Oregon. This last trick may be the scariest in the Barred's bag if the Spotted Owl proves, in fact, to be an endangered species.

Though we heard Barred Owls several times and in several states in the interim, it would be five years before we would actually *see* one. It was summertime, South Carolina, languid heat, heavy humidity. Predictably, we were on the swampy margins of a forest of trees with moss-festooned branches larger than most of the trees in Iowa. It was late afternoon and the sun was slipping down through an ethereal golden haze suffused with the sweet-sour redolence of multiple paper mills. Through the interplay of eerie light and torpid shadows, an owl conjured itself past us on silent wing and landed, inexplicably, on a nearby snag. A large owl. Dark-eyed. Barred. BARRED!

It watched us — graced us — for but a moment. Curiosity apparently assuaged, it slipped off as quietly as it had come into the murky labyrinth of swamp, leaving us to ponder the first corollary of owling and to question why we were now amongst the chosen. With owls one can never be sure. That night after dinner, I was stricken with some abominable eight-hour stomach flu that rendered me doubled up and sleepless the entire night. It left me, like the owl had, as quickly as it had come, to sleepwalk groggily through a terrible day of work.

Several times throughout the rest of that summer we saw Barred Owls, both in daylight and at dusk, though we never saw one that was calling. We heard Barreds throughout that summer, almost daily, during daytime and at night, though we could never entice a calling Barred to come see us. Never the rest of the entire summer was one of us sick for one minute. Dues apparently considered paid in full, the magician had allowed us an audience but never invited us behind the curtain.

Twenty years later I was sure I had at last stepped behind that curtain. I was in the Okanagan highlands of Canada with Dick Cannings, a biologist and lifelong owl researcher. It was autumn in British Columbia. A crisp chill air was so clear we could see mountains two hours south of us in Washington. We were deep in forests of larch and fir as the sun dropped behind a western plateau. This ecological niche of the world had absolutely nothing in common with that Carolina summer of so long ago… except for the Barred Owls. Dick and I had spent the warmth of the afternoon calling up Northern Pygmy-Owls, and intended to spend the rapidly-cooling evening calling up Boreal Owls.

While we waited for darkfall, he filled me in on recent owl counts done here in his home province. Spotted Owls were rare here, at the margins of their preferred habitat, and were declining because contiguous family groups were not prospering enough to fill the voids left by natural attrition. Barred Owls were not uncommon here, were prospecting into habitats apparently unsuitable for Spotteds — were, in short, expanding their range.

We stopped at a large dead snag along a logging road where, only days before, he and the group he was leading had seen a Barred Owl. I stepped behind a tree to urinate while Dick droned on about the nuances of calendar and clock, guesstimating our chances for seeing Boreals. For just a moment my mind drifted, attentive to the business at hand. Suddenly, with no warning, Crazy Owl's eight blood-curdling syllables boomed out from right behind me, swept over me, broadcast out in waves through the twilight, closer even than on that long-ago night in Iowa.

My head snapped around with a force that would have convulsed a lesser neck with severe whiplash. I peered

The Barred Owl's large, dark eyes and barred chest are distinctive. All other large North American owls, except the Barn Owl and the Spotted Owl, have yellow eyes.

around the tree seeking Dick's eyes in the just-enough remaining light to see where they were directed, so I could direct my own upon our sudden visitor. Dick's eyes were looking at me! He was grinning hugely. His resounding, full-throated "*Who cooks for you all*" would have been the envy of any Barred Owl I had ever encountered. For my part, he allowed that he had never seen any of the owls (legendary for their mythical ability to swivel the head a full 360) go 180 as quickly and smoothly as had I. Luckily for Dick, my pants were already open or we would have been trekking back to town before looking for Boreals.

We waited the requisite ten minutes to see if the magician would grant us an audience in response to Dick's calls. Every

The Barred Owl's feet are small when compared to a Great Horned Owl's; they are more suited to small prey such as voles, mice, and shrews. Because of their proximity to rivers, they also eat frogs, snakes, and crayfish.

Barred Owl

long-time birder has entertained the unspoken fantasy of a much-sought species being out there somewhere, watching the watcher. Though it would be hard to document, with all owls and with Barreds in particular, this fantasy typically ripens into delicious fact. The Barred is an illusionist capable of making itself appear and disappear, not in simple compliance with a spoken command, but in measured non-compliance with unspoken hopes. Here is an illusionist brash enough to attempt the disappearance of a whole other species of its own tribe. And hooting with raucous derision at every performance.

A Barred Owl never came to us that night, but I knew out there somewhere one was watching, taking notes. Dick's little charade would soon go down the owls' own hotline, would soon enter the bulging bag of tricks. Perhaps by the following summer the ruse would be perpetrated on birders, owlers, in woods and swamps all over North America. A new "war" story, perhaps repeated often enough to enter the realm of owling lore, perhaps a new corollary to Barred Owling 202. "You're not going to believe this, but I had just stepped behind a tree… luckily my fly was already open…"

Somewhere a barred owl is laughing raucously.

Barred Owl wing from above and below.

Chapter Three
Short-Eared Owl

The Short-Eared Owl is our most aerial owl, often abroad by daylight over any open expanse. A streaked tawny brown color and its irregular flopping flight identify it as it courses marshes, fields, and prairies in search of rodents. It is found nearly worldwide, and in North America, it breeds from the Arctic to the central United States.

The Priesthood of Light and Space

A NOTE ABOUT FIELD NOTES: This chapter of Short-eared Owl observations is taken from my field notes. Field notes are short, cryptic summaries, replete with the observer's own set of often seemingly-unintelligible abbreviations (for example, SEOW is the bird banders' four-letter code for Short-eared Owl), of the date and time a species was encountered, and any unusual circumstances defining that encounter. (Other abbreviations I've used in this chapter are explained on the next page.)Field notes are typically entered into a dog-eared, snack-stained, pocket notebook with a pencil crying out for sharpening. If the notebook has been forgotten, old envelopes and magazine tear-outs are used. One of the entries in this chapter was actually written with ball-point pen along the inside of my forearm.

Some birders will meticulously translate their field notes into the English language and/or into their computer when they arrive home. Most birders intend to do this but never get around to it.

As its name implies, the Short-eared Owl shows only small ear tufts that appear more as ridges and show when the owl is in a defensive posture.

Field Note Abbreviations

SEOW: Short-eared Owl

1: the number of individuals of the species observed

NWR: National Wildlife Refuge

Deva: my wife

Bumbles: our two young sons

Field notes serve two purposes. They provide permanent records (well, I did wash my arm) to help with planning future trips, and they are mementoes which years down the road may facilitate all manner of nostalgia, lies, confessions, and on occasion, even scientific research. Because I am a writer and writers have to write, the italicized paragraphs at the end of each entry are like editorials, which I always append to my field notes which then, accordingly, turn into field volumes. My pencils are forever blunt.

December 15, 1971; Squaw Creek NWR, MO: marsh along west side of perimeter; Deva & Jim; 8:30 a.m.; 1; cold, low ceiling, fixing to snow; ice on small ponds; Bald Eagle stooping on injured Snow Goose; SEOW coursing over marsh like harrier

The eagle has landed! Every time, time after time, the entire goose and duck population of the refuge arises, accompanied by an unbelievable cacophony of sound — anxious gabbling swelling to a raucous roar, drowning out wind, engine noise, conversation! Scoping alongside the main pond we see, then hear. Driving the perimeter, sound preceding the shimmering motion above the horizon, we hear, then see. What a rush! And an owl that seeks open space and broad daylight, surely a special, very different breed of owl!

November 3, 1975; Bellevue, WA: 108th NE & NE 8th; Deva & both bumbles; noon; 1; crisp; cloudy; SEOW flew through fog over meadow, harassed by ravens; finally landed on ground amidst dead grass tufts & stayed remainder of day

Owl down, ravens perch and wait. Owl up, ravens come. They own this air space over this meadow. The owl finally figures this out and stays down, probably goes to sleep. Ravens lose interest and go off to find a new game. Owl has nice, peaceful daytime roost.

November 8, 1975; Bellevue, WA: Bellefields Park; by myself; 10:30 a.m.; 1; crisp; cloudy; muskrats, deer; SEOW touched down twice, but immediately arose again and continued flopping along borders of muck & marsh

Could be our friend from the raven games. It has found ideal habitat here, thousands of treeless, open acres reclaimed from Lake Washington and preserved as a wild area. Seattle has to be the most natural urban area in the country.

May 15, 1976; Grant Co., WA: Columbia NWR; Deva & bumbles, Bert & Sylvia Jahn; 8 a.m.; 1; already warm, not a cloud in the sky; Red-tailed Hawk w/snake dangling from talons soaring to cliff nest; to initiates such as us, SEOW looks out of place here, cruising sagebrush

Jahns say the Short-eareds don't nest here in high desert, but actually the vast open expanses well fit their soaring, peripatetic huntstyle. This could be a transient going north or a resident from nearby agricultural areas watered by irrigation from the Columbia. One species' lost habitat is another's found.

February 6, 1977; Skagit Co., WA: Skagit Flats; Deva & bumbles; 10 a.m.; 1; cold, windy, intermittent mist; immature Bald Eagle flew directly over our heads on its way out to Snow Goose flock; SEOW made at least a dozen strikes but we never saw it score.

How many strikes, or what percentage of failed strikes, trigger an owl to leave seemingly viable habitat for better hunting grounds? Are humans that smart or does perseverance prevail over instinct? Much as I would hate to leave this beautiful part of the country, we may be out of here soon, seeking better hunting ground ourselves.

December 30, 1982; Anahuac NWR, TX: West Line Rd; Deva & both boys; 6 p.m.; 5; all day rain over at sundown; full moon rising up through mist; damp, spooky; howling bobcats; SEOWs like giant moths w/languorous, floppy-winged flight over spartina marshes

We've never seen multiple Short-eareds! We've never seen a bobcat! We've never even heard a bobcat! This was a pretty good day at the office!

Short-Eared Owl
Asio flammeus

Most frequently heard vocalization
Typically silent except in nesting season. A raspy, high-pitched barking is the alarm vocalization of both sexes.

Size
A medium-sized owl, approximately 15" long with a 38-40" wingspan; about the size of a crow

Most notable physical features
- round-headed; ear tufts usually not noticeable
- buffy, with boldly-streaked underparts
- bold buffy wing patches show in flight and on the underwing
- long, narrow wings
- easy, floating flight

Seasonal movement
Migratory; withdraws southward from Alaska and Canada into lower 48 states in winter

Nest sites
Depressions on the ground in dense grasses

Habits
Diurnal; usually seen coursing low over fields early and late in the day

Range/habitat
Short-eared Owls live in the open country of Alaska, Canada, and the northern half of the continental United States.

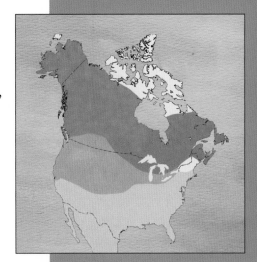

The Short-eared Owl is considered to be a highly migratory species, especially in the northern limits of its range. Banding data shows 1,000-mile movements in 50 days, although these movements can vary widely.

August 28, 1988; Stanislaus Co., CA; St. Rt. 120 east of Oakdale; Deva; 1 p.m.; <u>1</u>; hot, humid, sunny; SEOW working field along highway

Six years. It's been a long time. No accompaniment of other wildlife this time, but the high Sierras form a powerful backdrop. Maybe we are the Short-eareds of the human race: transients, fellow travelers, seeking wilderness, seeking distance, seeking space.

August 31, 1990; Wallowa Co., OR; I-84 S of LaGrande; Deva; 4 p.m.; <u>1</u>; cool, even in the sun, windy; SEOW working hayfield below highway level

On the road again. Dropping out of the Blue Range, Eagle Caps on our left, as far as eye can see there are pines, peaks, perfect valleys dotted by perfect ranches that seem to have sprung whole from the imagination of Louie L'Amour. In a tribe populated mostly by species that come and go in an eyeblink, prefer deep woods and close thickets, and inhabit the dark corners of our world and our minds, Short-eareds are a welcome anomaly. Buoyant and breezy, never in a hurry, but always going somewhere, Short-eareds convey vast distances. Short-eareds connote air and light and space.

June 13, 1992; St. Lawrence Is., AK; Gambell; Deva, Wings; 3 days; <u>10</u>; cold, windy, cloudy w/1 day of sunshine, no precip; Polar Bear skins drying on village rooftops, Red-legged Kittiwake Qed for group when I made initial SEOW sighting

Never a close look. The owls are no dummies. They know the village philosophy — if it flies, shoot it. Anything with wings is target practice. Who are the 'bird brains' here? Is it the birders, whom the natives have sarcastically labeled, or is it the natives? It ain't the owls. Most of the group is happy to have come, will be happier to leave. Gambell is a spooky place. Is it inbreeding, is it alcohol and drugs, or is it just the expected residue of a hunting culture hung up halfway up/down the spiral to "civilization"?

June 18, 1992; Nome, AK; out the Kougarock and along Safety Sound; Deva, Sue Utterback, Charlotte Mathena; <u>4</u>; sunny, windy; bugs tolerable, dust intolerable; 1st SEOW sighting between road & small Musk Oxen herd being stalked by

Short-eared Owl

Grizzly Bear; owls prospecting tundra & along beaches around gold dredges

The Short-eared's mystique continues to grow! Wherever Short-eareds roam, long desired, highly sought, very special species are always found.

December 11, 1992; Laveen, AZ; 1/4 mi S. of Dobbins on 59th Ave; Steve, Roy, Anita, Bix, Liz, Cindy; 8:30 a.m.; 1 (8 & 4 seen on 2 previous days); sunny, chilly, dewy after fog lifted; SEOW flushed out of alfalfa field near lambing sheep; elevated above wires & floated out of sight

Mystique? Lambing sheep? Actually there seem to be many reports of Short-eareds near lambing sheep. Is it the afterbirth or just the rodents kicked up by the sheep and/or attracted to the sheep droppings? It's a wonder we haven't heard some sheepmen claiming owls are killing newborn lambs. After all, sheepmen and cattlemen are close kin, both superfluous middlemen in the nutrition transfer from land to gut, through wasteful and damaging intermediaries.

November 28, 1993; Skagit Co., WA: Samish Flats; Deva; 9:30 a.m.; 1; cloudy, light drizzle; checkerboard of ag fields a raptor convention in winter; SEOW flew under utility pole crossbar sporting live Gyrfalcon!

Snowy Owl, multiple Rough-leggeds, preening Peregrine on another pole — have we missed anything!? There is an old man on an even older bicycle between us and the Gyr pole. We catch up, pass, stop and get out to scope. He passes us, flushes Gyr. We catch up, pass, stop and get out to scope. He passes us, flushes Gyr. For miles! We can't stop to explain for fear we'll lose track of the Gyr. Old man probably won't stop because of the rain. Gyr won't stop because there are no bicycles or vans in the land of its birth. Meanwhile, the Short-eared blithely follows, three feet off the ground, stooping, retracing, flopping along like a tortoise keeping the three hares in sight.

July 4, 1994; Glennallen, AK: Deva; 6:30 a.m.; 1; sunny, cool; morning run along Glenn Highway, just west of town; passed moose browsing willow thicket; SEOW broke across highway in front of us from bog area

Short-eared Owls in the wild have reached almost 13 years of age. Natural enemies include raptors such as the Bald Eagle, Northern Goshawk, Gyr Falcon, Red-tailed Hawk and Snowy Owl. Because they nest on the ground, they are vulnerable to mammalian predators such as skunks, foxes, and coyotes. Collisions with vehicles account for a large number of deaths, and because they are attracted to the wide open fields of airports, many are killed by collisions with aircraft.

At midmorning we queue up waiting for the Independence Day
Parade to pass along Glennallen's four block Main Street. Everyone
gets out of their vehicles and ambles around exchanging this and that.
The driver of a service truck points to the thicket where we had seen
the moose while we were running, and says how he had seen a grizzly cross the highway at that exact spot earlier in the morning — at
6:45! Perhaps we need to rethink our long-term relationship with the
owl of light and space!

November 5, 1994; Santa Cruz Co., AZ: Vaca Corral, San
    Rafael Grasslands; Deva, Charlie Babbitt; 11 a.m.; 1; sunny;
    cold breeze moving the grasses & windmills; herd of ante-
    lope watched us watch SEOW; owl flushed over next hill
    every time we broke ridgeline
It looks good now with nothing but grass and windmills rolling to the
foot of the distant Huachucas, but imagine what it looked like before
the Texans brought their cattle and the grasses were waist high.
Short-eareds are not as common here as you would expect. Like us,
they probably preferred it before the cattle outnumbered the antelope.

June 10, 1995; Glenn Highway, AK; mile pt. 146; Deva; 1; 7:30
    a.m.; cool, unbelievably clear; looks like we could reach out
    and touch Wrangells on eastern skyline; life Northern
    Hawk Owl late last night on way from Anchorage; SEOW
    came out of stunted willow bog and nearly collided with
    moving car
We have already seen four Hawk Owls today! Where were they in
'94 when we spent a week looking to no avail? That's the trouble
with Short-eareds as with other conjurers and sorcerers. You can
never know what ingredients are thrown into the brew. This year
voles are the main ingredient. A ranger tells us there are so many
this year he has seen them crossing the highway in daylight, unprece-
dented in his many years in Alaska.

In flight, the Short-eared Owl can be confused with
the Northern Harrier, but the Short-eared Owl's head
is larger, and its wingbeats are stiffer. Additionally,
the Short-eared Owl's flight is distinctively moth-like

The Short-eared Owl nests and roosts on the ground. Its preferred habitats include open prairies, coastal grasslands, tundra, marshes, bogs, savanna, and dunes.

<u>February 8, 1997</u>; Elmore Co., ID; ST Rt 20 east of Mountain Home; Deva, Bud Johnson; 5:30 p.m.; <u>1</u>; clear, cold, sundown; heading for Boise after Siberian Accentor chase, we had seen a brown morph Gyr near Ketchum; SEOW floated across highway over top of car, landed on metal culvert post w/orange reflector; Bud whipped car around as I scrambled for camera

This is as close as we've ever been to a Short-eared and the longest one has ever sat for us. Bud is driving. He watches, slack-jawed, as I bail out of the passenger seat, drop to my knees on the still-warm pavement of the deserted highway, and bow before the owl. From thirty feet I thank it for the accentor and the Gyr. I thank it for these telephotos, I thank it for this audience, I thank it for life. Had Bud known tomorrow would bring his life Gray Partridge, he would have been on his knees right there beside me.

<u>July 2, 1998</u>; Churchill, MB; old town beach; Deva; 7:30 a.m.; <u>1</u>; cool, windy, partial overcast; we stopped on RR tracks to glass gull gang down on shore; we would find 2(!) Ross's this morning, but we see SEOW coming toward us first; by time we get glasses up it is too close to focus; veers off behind rental truck 10 ft from us; we thought it was coming in through window!

By now we should expect a close Short-eared encounter to preclude something portentous. One Ross' we have seen every other day for a week. This day we notice the bird doesn't seem as deep a pink. Perhaps it's the light. A Peregrine puts them up, scrambling all the puzzle pieces. The flock resettles. We refind a very pink bird. We glance at one another, wide-eyed. We swing the glasses back and sweep again, very slowly this time. They are both there! Short-eared magic.

<u>January 9, 1999</u>; Cochise Co., AZ: Meadow Valley Rd, San Rafael Grasslands; by myself; 7 p.m.; <u>1</u>; clear, cold; past sundown; a three-quarter moon is rising behind Bog Hole windmill; prior to this SEOW I have seen nothing today worth recording; as this spectral being levitates away into deepening darkness, I know absolutely that tomorrow I will.

The creaking of the windmill awakens me at first light. I crawl from the bag and look to the east. A breeze touches my face. The Huachuca

crest is a sharp silhouette across miles and
miles of moving grass. Vast distance.
Space. The peaks of the
Patagonias are behind me,
awash in first light. The windmill creaks again. I look up.
The blades are moving,
ever so slowly. On the
supporting metalwork behind
the blades sits a small falcon,
with large, perfect, chocolate hearts
running up flanks and across midriff. It is an
immature Prairie Falcon, perhaps a male judging by the
size. A blade slowly throws him into shadow, then hides
him altogether. Then he reappears in the interval
between blades, like some shy schoolboy
not quite sure if he should watch
nor if he should himself be
seen. I grin up at him, invite
myself to breakfast, and walk
up under the windmill with
my telephoto lens. I am having cold cereal. He is having
warm mouse, evidently caught
moments before. He has learned well. I
compliment him. We exchange a few pleasantries.
I snap his picture. We speak of our love for these high, lonesome grasslands. I ask if he knows God to be a Short-eared Owl. He
seems uncomfortable with the concept, unsure of how to answer. It is
all right, I say — probably He is not, but surely God and Short-eareds
are on a first-name basis. I am off to look for Baird's Sparrows and
Sprague's Pipits. He is off to master the wind. We both know that
somewhere out there is a fellow traveler, watching as we enjoy his vast
and spacious domain.

Short-eared Owl wing from
above and below.

Chapter Four

Snowy Owl

The Snowy Owl has the greatest average weight of all the North American owls, and is believed to be the most powerful. It inhabits the northern tundra around the world, living in areas of low, sparse vegetation, open fields, valley floors, and salt and poorly-drained fresh water meadows. Its habitat is closely associated with the distribution of small rodents, especially lemmings.

The Dance of Life

WESTWARD, TO OUR LEFT, looming up surreally through the thick, unbroken fog bank stretched out at our feet for forty miles, were the glistening, ice-laden peaks of some Siberian mountain chain, foreboding and unfathomable in their geographic and psychological isolation. Eastward, to our right, perhaps a mile away through the mists rising from the plateaued headlands' tundra grasses, the struggle amongst the tufts and hummocks ended predictably. A Snowy Owl, a young female wearing "headsets," appeared in the Questar atop a spire of rock. Tipping back her head, she gulped the rodent down head first, its tail hanging from her beak until the end. Gaping twice, she then sat, satiated, and preened for us. It was perfect, this encounter with a spectral owl here at the absolute ends of the earth.

The Snowy Owl, the largest of our owls (at least in body size and weight if not in actual wingspan) is also the most powerful.

The Snowy Owl's nesting season is May through September. The young can walk at about two weeks of age, and leave the nest when they are 20-30 days old, but are still unable to fly. They do not master flying until they are about 50 days old.

Eclectic feeders, though usually taking the lemmings and mice most plentiful on their arctic breeding tundra, they have been known to pluck ptarmigan from the ground with one taloned foot! They will take geese. They will eat carrion. They will eat fish. As with all of our owls, the Snowy's opportunistic bent often belies the myths and romanticism that have grown around it from ancient times to modern.

A family of Snowy Owls is painted on a cave wall in the Dordogne region of France, thought to be the earliest representation of bird by man. Paleolithic Man left the cave a reliquary from the past, the ancient owl surely seeking far-away rodents in long-ago tundra along the margins of time-forgotten ice. We saw our first Snowy perched on an international orange hi-loader in the middle of the University of Washington campus in the middle of Seattle. The next day it was hunting a shard of terraced landscaping in the snarl of a nearby freeway cloverleaf.

THIS SECOND SNOWY, near Gambell at the northwest end of St. Lawrence Island in the Bering Sea, more closely matched the bird with its mystique.

No one comes to Gambell for Snowy Owl. Morning sea watches at the point had already produced "Spectacular" Eider and Common Ringed Plover for our group, and the cry of "Ross's Gull!" the previous evening had cleared the dining area faster than would have the Second Coming.

This morning, after breakfast, we had slogged the two miles of loose cobbles from the village to the "mountain" with Eurasian Dotterel on our minds. The gradual, mile-long ascent from sea level to tundra on the huge plateau overlooking the coastal village is made only by special permission from Aleut elders, for near the top lies the village "cemetery." Permafrost dictates the bodies of the deceased be placed here in a series of caves rather than interred beneath the frozen soil.

The Snowy Owl is perhaps one of the few among the owl tribes not particularly associated in folklore with fear, omen, and death. Still it seemed somehow appropriate that we should find our snowy (but no Eurasian Dotterel) after passing discomfitingly close to the open gravesites, some displaying native crosses and decorative amulets.

We were out of our element. We had entered the realm of the great white owl of the great white north. The polar bear skins, stretched and drying on the village rooftops, were proof enough. This was a dichromatic world, with only shades of gray and muted browns, a world of vast distances with no use for the calibrations of time we bore on our wrists. Despite the promise of Asian vagrants still to come, those of us for whom the preening female in the scope was a

Snowy Owl
Nyctea scandiaca

Most frequently heard vocalization
Typically silent; high, thin, drawn-out scream in territorial disputes

Size
Very large, approximately 23" long with a 52-60" wingspan; our heaviest owl, it averages about 4 pounds

Most notable physical features
• large, white owl with sparse dark speckling
• round head, yellow eyes
• some birds are much whiter than others
• smooth plumage
• perches prominently in open areas

Seasonal movement
Irruptive movement of younger birds southward in winter into northern half of continental U.S. in years when prey species decline.

Nest sites
Scrapes and depressions on boulders and raised areas of tundra

Habits
Diurnal

Range/habitat
Northernmost regions of Alaska and Canada; winters sporadically far south to central U.S. in irruption years. Habitat includes prairies, fields, marshes, beaches, dunes, and the Arctic tundra in summer.

Snowy Owl

lifer were ecstatic. With a final shrug of displaced feathers, she left her spire of rock and flew off above the fog bank shrouding the Bering Sea. Though certainly not seen in our Questar view, it was no great leap of imagination to know she had blood on her beak and carried the genetic memory of ancestors who had coursed the ancient land bridge, just to our north, from whence had come the harbingers of our civilization.

In six months this young female might be on the Samish Flats of Washington or in the Flint Hills of Kansas, the Snowy and the lemming being inextricable partners in the dance of life. The cyclical crash in northern rodent populations sends this species

Opposite: The Snowy Owl is almost totally silent outside its breeding grounds. Above: Snowy Owls have a direct, strong, and steady flight with deliberate, powerful down-strokes and quick upstrokes. They make short flights, close to the ground, from perch to perch.

south during "invasion" years, younger birds displaced the far-thest in their search for prey. It is these displaced winter birds that most birders encounter as their first Snowy, usually bearing more brown speckling and spotting than older birds who have successfully defended territories closer to their Arctic domain.

The purist in me wishes our life Snowy Owl had been an old male, pure white, perhaps defending a nest, perhaps purveying rodents to a mate with nestlings atop a tundra heave north of the Arctic Circle. But Snowies, as have we, have come long and far from the land bridge — hi-loaders on a university campus; grain elevators near open winter waters; traffic reflectors on lower

The Snowy Owl's range has cyclic winter irruptions into the northern United States when there is a drastic decline in the number of lemmings, its chief prey, in its Arctic home. Individuals seen far to the south of its normal range are often starved and stressed for food, and thus active in daylight.

Adult female Snowy Owls are much more heavily barred and noticeably larger than adult males, who can be entirely white except for a few dark spots or bars on the crown, back, wings, and tail. The Snowy's dull black bill is almost buried in its fluffy white feathers.

forty-eight jetways. We enjoy other families of birds variously for their beautiful plumage, their migratory feats, their structural adaptations, their incomparable vocalizations. It seems only with the owls that we use terms like "evoke" and "conjure."

Owls run deep into our psyche, into our very souls. The Snowy Owl, visiting from its remote high-arctic desert vastnesses, running in its timeless rhythms of scarcity and plenty, brings to us visceral remembrances of a relationship with the natural world from which our species evolved. Here in our postmodern "civilization," here in our scurried element, we need these cyclical

Snowy Owl

reminders of whence we came. And we need to know, if only vicariously, that the realm of grays and muted browns, where the sun never sets on the intricate choreography of rodent and owl, is still there. To remember less, to know less, is to mark our extinction as an evolved species. The great white owl remembers where and when. The great white owl *is* where and when.

Snowy Owl wing from above and below.

Chapter Five

Spotted Owl

The Spotted Owl is arguably the most well-known owl in America, sitting quietly at the center of the environment-versus-development controversy. In this chapter, facts, figures, and opinions in the non-italicized paragraphs are extrapolated from my field notes (uh... field volumes). Facts, figures, opinions, and the words of Mark Twain found in the italicized paragraphs are extrapolated from articles on the Spotted Owl (sources appear at the end of the chapter).

American Icon

THE NEXT TIME YOU'RE enviously contemplating the glamour and privilege bestowed on an American celebrity, consider the price: strangers roaming your neighborhood to discover where and how you live; quiet meals after dark interrupted by prying eyes and flashing lights; public reporting of the most intimate details of your sex life; stalkers who seek the cachet of being able to say simply that they have seen you.

As recently as 1968, in the entire state of Oregon, the epicenter of the Spotted Owl controversy, there had been only two-dozen sightings of this bird. Today, after two decades of the "owl wars," the Spotted Owl is the most widely-studied and well-known owl on the planet.

We saw our first Spotted Owl near Old Blewett Pass on the east slope of Washington's Cascade range in July, 1976. The Spotted Owl was placed on the Endangered Species List in June, 1980. We knew this owl when this owl wasn't cool. That's cachet!

The Spotted Owl is a forest owl, and a cousin to the Barred Owl. The two species are very similar, both with brown plumage, dark eyes, and barking calls.

Since its inclusion on "the list" in the early 1980s the Spotted Owl has become the icon of the environmentalist movement, polarizing old growth forest conservationists and the nation's logging industry, their litigious confrontation overshadowing the bird itself.

Our second Spotted Owl encounter, in Arizona's Pinaleno Mountains in late October, 1985, was an aural encounter on a moonless fall night black as a witch's cape, in which we never glimpsed the bird but heard enough of its bizarre vocal repertoire to completely buy into the most terrifying gothic myths of Halloween. The words I find in my logbook are "hissing screams, mewing, and the barking of baying hounds" — a ten-minute cacophony triggered by the chance dropping of a metal pot against a rock as we cleaned up our campsite prior to retiring for the night. The owl could only have been in the huge Ponderosa above our tent, startled as much by us as we by it. Needless to say, we did not drop off immediately into peaceful slumber.

There are those on both sides of the debate who firmly believe the Spotted Owl is neither rare nor even endangered, but simply a convenient and timely surrogate for old growth survival, grasped by the "tree huggers" eager for a cause in their fight with the forest industries.

The next morning, as Deva led single file on a steep hiking trail from our campsite into a nearby canyon, I watched a copious wad of whitewash drop from above and miss her head by inches. Our previous night's poltergeist was on a limb, directly above the trail, slumbering peacefully. We would neither have spotted it nor even looked up from the rocky, uneven trail had the bird not chosen that precise moment to defecate.

Which of these two official statistics would be the easiest to derive and the most likely accurate — the actual number of Spotted Owls in the Pacific Northwest or the actual number of jobs lost to the moratorium on forest logging due to the owl issue? Both of these contentious debates remind one of Mark Twain's famous line about "lies, damned lies, and statistics."

Since that memorable weekend in the Pinalenos, our experiences with this owl, though more frequent, have become most routine and unremarkable. As is so often the case in our culture, the Spotted Owl did not achieve its celebrity status until it had become a mediagenic darling created by political controversy. It seems as though the ensuing public scrutiny stripped from this species the aura and mystique associated with the less well known members of its tribe, indeed stripped away its "personality."

In the late 1980s, a committee of owl experts concluded that a minimum population of 1,500 pairs of Spotted Owls in Washington, Oregon, and California must be maintained to preserve the species. By the mid 1990s, 2,100 pairs and hundreds of single birds had been tallied in Washington and Oregon alone.

Spotted Owl
Strix occidentalis

Most frequently heard vocalization
4 syllables, "Hoo, hoo-hoo, hooo." Loud but short, resembling barking; similar to barred owl, but a shorter "who, cooks, for, you-OU!" with longer pauses

Size
A large owl, 18" long with a 40" wingspan; slightly smaller than barred owl, but with similar proportions

Most notable physical features
• round head with no ear tufts
• dark underparts with white spots
• dark eyes

Seasonal movement
Sedentary with some altitudinal migration in winter

Nest sites
Broken tree top platforms; tree and cliff cavities; mistletoe brooms

Habits
Nocturnal but occasionally found on daytime roosts

Range/habitat
Pacific coast, central Sierras; central to southern Arizona and New Mexico; the two populations of Spotted Owls do not overlap in their range, differing only in plumage. The Pacific Spotted Owls are darker overall than the interior west Spotted Owls. Their habitat consists of mountain canyons with old growth conifer stands.

Wild and crazy anecdotes — a staple of birders searching for other owls — are seldom heard in conjunction with Spotted Owls. There are reasons for this. One is simply that during the birding boom of the 1980s and early 1990s, casual birders were fearful of venturing into Spotted Owl habitat on the west coast, afraid they might literally become statistics in a "war" real enough that Spotted Owl carcasses festooned many a rural fenceline and back-roads bar.

Approximately 15,000 timber industry jobs have been lost in Oregon, but the Cascades have hardly become the "Appalachia of the West" as was predicted. Oregon's unemployment rates have fallen below the national level and timber prices have increased due to public lands taken out of forest production. Logging companies have been forced to replant after decades of neglect, mills have automated, forest management has become flexible and innovative, and a value-added wood industry has mushroomed.

Friends of ours vacationing on the Olympic Peninsula during the height of the "owl wars" discovered every pick-up on the road bore some Spotted Owl-related bumper aphorism, none favorable, the most popular an owl caricature superimposed by a bullseye. Our friends were warned before touring the area to remove Audubon Society and Nature Conservancy stickers from their vehicle window. A typical celebrity, the Spotted Owl — beloved by some segments of society, vilified by others.

It all began when studies indicated that the Spotted Owl has a very narrow thermal neutral zone, rendering this species highly susceptible to heat stress. During daytime it thermoregulates under the forest canopy by seeking roost sites in optimal microclimates. Thus, an early hypothesis of Spotted Owl research was that the species required old-growth forests to avoid heat stress.

A corollary reason for the dearth of Spotted Owl search sagas is that most birders figured sooner or later they would see "Smitty's" owls in Arizona. When Robert T. "Smitty" Smith died in August, 1998, it was guesstimated he had guided over 7,000 people into Arizona's Huachuca Mountains to see the Scheelite

Canyon Spotted Owls. And for every one of those, there were probably ten others who knew of these birds and made the pilgrimage on their own only because of his lifelong devotion to them. Undoubtedly, a majority of those who have recorded this species saw Smitty's birds first.

Forest type, if nothing else, seems to prove three distinct subspecies of Spotted Owl, one in the firs of the Pacific Northwest, one in the redwoods of northern California, and a third in the Ponderosa canyons of the Southwest, which include the birds of southern California and Arizona.

In 1986, prior to our first trip to Yosemite, I spoke long distance with an avid northern California birder we had met on an pelagic trip out of Monterey. An article in a birding magazine indi-

The Spotted Owl's diet is 90 percent small mammals, including flying squirrels, wood rats, rabbits, bats, mice, and moles. They will also eat other birds, snakes, crickets, beetles, and moths.

Spotted Owls are distinguished from Barred Owls by a smaller size and a darker overall appearance.

cated Spotted Owls could be found within an hour of her home. We thought it would be cachet to say we had seen all three subspecies. My inquiry was met with a long pause followed by a grudging admission — "I've never seen a Spotted Owl in California. The only ones I've ever seen were the ones in Scheelite."

Some of the highest Spotted Owl densities were discovered on land owned and logged by Simpson Timber in the redwood country of northern California. Only two percent of this land was old growth. Clearcutting, anathema to forest conservationists, seems logical in redwoods which have the ability to sprout new growth directly from cutover stumps and their roots. Stump sprouting, moreover, is enhanced by full sunlight. Second growth redwoods can reach 150 feet in only fifty years!

Perhaps the Spotted Owl lacks the aura and mystique of other owls, not because of its celebrity status, but despite it. In 1987 we took the hike with Smitty to see "his" owls for the first time. We found the birds, the pair of them side by side on a low, horizontal branch, sleeping. Since then, in nearly two-dozen sightings in various canyons in various mountain ranges throughout Arizona, the only thing we have seen Spotted Owls do besides sleep is sidle sideways up branches to escape from sunshaft back into shade.

There is growing evidence that sprouting redwood stumps provide ideal habitat for the Spotted Owl's two primary prey species in redwood areas, the wood rat and the brush rabbit. In old growth, the populations of these two species decline dramatically.

During the Eared Trogon (a beautiful Mexican bird rarely seen north of the border) furor in the Huachucas in the fall of 1991, we went on a day that a pair of Spotteds was discovered roosting near the trail from the top of Carr Canyon. Birders from California, Wisconsin, and Britain were happy to add this pair to their life lists, but not ecstatic. Ecstasy they reserved solely for the trogon sighting, as if years of reading about the owls' plight, and this pair's seeming insouciance to their discovery, had jaded the discoverers to the pleasures of this species and the singularity of stumbling upon it on their own outside of Scheelite.

In 1989 Pacific Lumber punched a logging road through the heart of a well-studied male's territory. Radio telemetry provided scientists with definitive data on "Luke" who stayed his course despite bulldozers, crashing trees, and typical logging commotion. He and his mate produced one offspring the following year, two in the year after.

Political writers, exempt from charges of anthropomorphism and uninitiated to the joys and frights of searching for owls in their primary habitat (which is to say the dead of night), often characterize the Spotted Owl as "retiring and shy." The spotteds along the trogon trail that day were nothing short of comatose. One observer slipped on rock rubble

Spotted Owls are long-lived, with birds in the wild reaching 16-17 years. For juveniles, however, mortality is very high (60-95 percent). Natural predators of the Spotted Owl include the Great Horned Owl, the Red-tailed Hawk, and the Common Raven, which destroys eggs.

and rolled raucously downslope through dry leaf litter and crackling dead branches to a stop literally at the owls' feet. No head perking, no neck swiveling, certainly no flushing. One bird somnolently opened its eyes, gaped a few times (resembling nothing so much as a big yawn), then returned to slumber. It's mate didn't even open its eyes!

The Spotted Owl is not a prolific species, reproducing at a very slow rate. Viability as a species requires a high survival rate. Present estimates place the percentage of juvenile birds surviving to maturity at 12 to 19 percent. Obviously, small changes could have great impacts.

Owls are variously seen as fearsome (Great Horned), humorous (Burrowing), scary (Barn), or endearing (Saw-Whet). If the "retiring and shy" Spotted Owl may be ascribed a personality, it would appear to be a studied or perhaps resigned indifference to the tumult in the owl woods these past two decades. Our most lasting impression, if distilled to one word, would be... sleepy. The clueless journalists may have the final word on this reclusive celebrity, after all.

The latest threat to the species is the invasion of its territory by the Barred Owl, a close but distinct relative from eastern forests. Barred Owls were first documented in the Pacific Northwest in the 1960s and in northern California in the 1990s. The Barred Owl apparently requires a less specialized forest niche, reproduces more rapidly, and has a higher survival rate.

As technology has replaced trees in the booming Pacific Northwest economy, future generations of birders may come to know the Spotted Owl, not simply as the black-and-white symbol of the green cause, but as a reason to go themselves into the spooky old woods. But then again, maybe they won't, for the nat-

Before their flight feathers are fully developed, young Spotted Owls leave the nest and perch on nearby branches. They often fall to the ground, but soon climb up nearby trees to perch. At 40-45 days old, most owlets can fly short distances.

ural history of the Spotted Owl seems to have been irrevocably complicated by this new interloper in the neighborhood.

Barreds and Spotteds are known to have mated and produced young, "Sparred Owls," which themselves seem capable of reproduction. Thus the Spotted Owl has become a victim of the subtlest but most devastating invasion — genetic invasion from within its own tribe. This gives fuller and truer meaning to the term "owl wars."

On our most recent trip to the Pacific Northwest, we camped along the Colonial Creek drainage on the west slope of the Cascades, hoping to add a new owl to our Washington state list. We had no luck, but the campground host couldn't believe we hadn't been awakened by the caterwauling that night of "his" resident poltergeist — a Barred Owl!

Here's what we have learned about species preservation from the Spotted Owl affair: solutions are complex, not simple; results will be incremental, not dramatic; outcomes may be impacted by factors unexpected and/or beyond our control.

So now an American icon that helped rewrite the lexicon of conservation and ecology for a whole generation of scientists, wilderness lovers, and wannabes, may already be near that final stage of celebrity cycle which passes from "What's a Spotted Owl?" to "Let's find a Spotted Owl" to "Let's find something similar to a Spotted Owl" to "What's a Spotted Owl?" Something tells me this reluctant luminary, still and always seeking shade and avoiding heat and light, will welcome any respite from the glaring limelight that has splayed for two decades through its cool and secluded canyons.

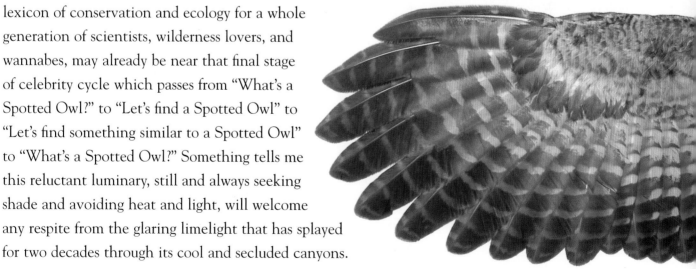

Spotted Owl wing from above and below.

Italicized excerpts were drawn from the following publications: *Audubon*, March, 1987; *Audubon*, March, 1991; *Backpacker*, December, 1981; *BioScience*, January, 1992; *Birds Of North America*, Academy of Natural Science of Philadelphia,1995; *National Geographic*, September, 1990; *National Review*, March 2, 1992; *National Wildlife*, August-September, 1995

Chapter Six

Eastern Screech-Owl

Eastern Screech-Owls come in two color phases, red and gray. Red individuals predominate across the mid-latitudes of their range from Missouri and Arkansas eastward. Gray forms are more common elsewhere. Their extremely nocturnal habits have added to the screech owl lore, which includes the belief that a sighting is an omen of misfortune or death.

The Escort

JIM!

My mother's voice, calling from the Midwest. And the surprise was the surprise and delight in that voice. My mother, by anyone's accounting, was now elderly. Early-in-life personal tragedy, years of loneliness, and recent major health issues had conspired to preclude, certainly not her will to live, but any joy she could find in that living. Years had passed since I had heard this spring in her voice.

Jim! I had an owl come to my bedroom windowsill late last night!

Combining geography with her rudimentary yet enthusiastic description — *could have held it in my hand… ears sticking straight up… all gray with big yellow eyes* — "her" owl could only have been an Eastern Screech-Owl. If my mother could be called a nature lover, she loved to love it from afar — books, calendars, television specials. A Victorian upbringing and an overwrought sense of neatness and personal cleanliness as an adult had con-

Though much smaller, Eastern Screech-Owls resemble Great Horned Owls both because of their "ear tufts," and because of their generalized diet and hunting skills.

spired to preclude, certainly not her fascination and appreciation of nature's beauty, but any inclination to delve too deeply into the harsh realities usually underlying that beauty.

So, my mother was definitely not a field birder. If she could be termed a "birder" at all, she was a feeder-watcher without the feeders. One of my earliest childhood memories was running down the long hallway to the back screened porch to discover the object of her exclamations was a flock of cedar waxwings feeding in the neighbors' Pyracantha.

LIKE ALL BIRD ENTHUSIASTS, my mother had her war stories, her finest being the recounting of the dinner party she and my father had thrown for his senior officers in the Seventh Cavalry stationed at Fort Bliss near El Paso in the 1930s. After an unsuccessful quail hunt, the sole purpose of which was to provide the entrée for this formal occasion, my father had returned home with several crows that he had shot, obviously legal game in Texas at the time. Between them they decided to use these birds in their favorite game recipe, hoping their guests would never realize they were… eating crow! Somehow, they pulled off this grand caper with straight faces, and her legendary reputation as a game cook continued to grow amongst their army friends.

But there had never been any owl stories. For the most part, you have to work at owls. Owls don't come to you. As my mother prattled on about the owl that had come to her window, my mind wandered off to cursor through my own experiences with Eastern Screech-Owls. It was a short file. Oddly enough, though I had grown up in the Midwest and begun birding there as a young adult, I could count my observations of Eastern Screech-Owl on one hand, with even a finger left over if one didn't count the road kill I had chanced upon in our two-year sojourn in Arkansas. This was attributable in part to having lived mostly in the West, and in part to screech owls being more difficult to find in the dense and verdant eastern forests relative to the wide open spaces of the west.

Not only were my sightings of some of the supposedly rarer and more difficult westerly and northerly owls more numerous than my Eastern Screech-Owl records, but I realized my only four screech owl sightings in the East had simply been owl caricatures, as it were. Three in Texas (two at Bentsen, one at Santa Ana) and one at Pelee, my four sightings were two-dimensional Eastern Screech-Owl icons placed by the birding gods in the requisite tree cavities in the requisite birding locations. Perhaps an eyeblink here and there, perhaps an icy stare, but no movement, no territorial calling, nor could I even claim to have been the original discoverer of these birds. My mother, with no mud on her boots, no briar scratches on her arms, and no sweat rings on her camouflage, had chanced upon her own Eastern Screech — a nocturnal, vocalizing, head-swiveling, three-dimensional eastern screech.

I ACCEDED TO A MOMENT of jealousy, ruminating on the scientific literature of the screech owls, eastern and western. "The little wildcats of the night," miniature killing machines, scaled-down versions of the Great Horned Owls known as "tigers of the night," the screech owls will take anything up to and sometimes greater than their own size, which is American Robin size. They are as widespread, within their range, as the Great Horned, and their range covers the entire lower forty-eight with the exception of

Most frequently heard vocalization
Long, descending whinny; they also deliver a mournful, even-toned trill, and when agitated, the piercing scream that gave them their name.

Size
A small owl, 7"-9" long, with a 20" wingspan; they are approximately the size of a cardinal or robin.

Most notable physical features
• red and gray color phases
• prominent ear tufts
• young birds may lack conspicuous ears
• light underparts with heavy streaking and weak barring
• pale bill, yellow eyes

Seasonal movement
Non-migratory; permanent resident

Nest sites
Tree cavities; lofts and niches of farm buildings; will use nest boxes

Habits
Extremely nocturnal

Range/habitat
Eastern screech-owls are found throughout forests, woodlots, and wooded urban areas of the eastern U.S., except for Maine.

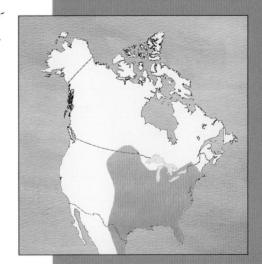

Maine, but because of their diminutive size they are much harder to find and observe despite their relative abundance.

The Eastern Screech-Owl is dimorphic, gray phase predominating in the north and in south Texas, red phase in the south. My four birds had all been gray, so red-phase Eastern Screech was still very near the top of my "want owl" list. Grays and reds have been known to mate and one can imagine the mindset of the first-time observer of such a pair until both are seen together. Such stories have only added to the "other" owl literature, the non-scientific literature of owls, a literature full of allusions to darkness and death.

To a twenty-first century birder, such associations may not seem reasonable, but stand in a dark woods and hear the quavering tremolo of a calling Eastern Screech-Owl and see if the mind doesn't blink, the skin on the back of the neck begin to crawl. For fourteen consecutive summer nights in Arkansas we stood on our back deck, extending into deep woods, and listened to this mournful, softly-descending wail, never seeing the bird, never able to shine it, never able to find it in extensive lighttime searches for its day roost.

My first three sightings of Eastern Screech-Owl were anticlimactic, simply chancing upon a fellow birder who had chanced upon a day roost, led me by the hand, shown me the motionless, sleeping owl sitting half exposed in a cavity opening. The fourth sighting, which began in a prosaically enough similar way, turned out to be dramatically different.

A birding acquaintance, a veteran of countless rambles through Bentsen State Park in Texas, offered to show me a screech owl he had found to be reliable at a specific site. Why not? After all, Bentsen is one of those deliciously anticipatory North American birding sites like Hugh Taylor Birch in Florida and the Patagonia Rest Area in Arizona where some drop-dead vagrant is always expected around the next turn in the trail. My friend led me off trail perhaps a quarter mile to a relatively open area in the thorn scrub forest, twisting and turning so that I knew I would never refind the place on my own.

Eastern Screech-Owls typically nest in tree hollows or niches of buildings, but they will also use nest boxes.

Playing his wizard's role to the hilt and enjoying every moment of it, he stopped me in a chaparral thicket replete with tangles of live vegetation, dead snags, and blowdowns. "It's here. See if you can find it," he grinned at me. I rolled my eyeballs and grinned back in wry appreciation of his spot-on understanding of what makes birders tick. Everything we could see was within twenty yards of our position. I left the binoculars hanging around my neck. A cursory glance around the perimeter revealed nothing but that eerie extrasensory perception of "something out there" watching you which can't itself be seen. And this in bright sunshine of mid-morning.

I started over, first inventorying the most obvious, and counted four cavities. None had an exposed owl at its opening. All had within their shadowed inner recesses that splotched and scaled stippling effect of weathered wood in which the owl-starved novice hole searcher always sees his bird but soon learns that longer, critical study always reveals nothing more than weathered wood. From these owl-less holes I moved on to close scrutiny of owl-less tangled vines, owl-less mistletoe clumps, and owl-less crotches of owl-less standing small trees.

Five owl-less minutes had passed. I glanced at Scott. He was still wearing his owlish grin, he and the owl now full partners in this little charade which could only end with me feeling like the volunteer from the audience at a travelling magic show. I raised the binoculars to my eyes and began anew. The first cavity was in the bole of a living tree, and through the glasses I could see that the spotting and cross-hatching I had seen with my naked eye was, indeed… spotting and cross-hatching on the inside of the bole.

The second cavity was eye level near the top of the standing stump of an ancient deadfall, thoroughly rotten and decayed inside. The hole, which faced us, was "V" shaped, opening out at the top and fragmenting into a wild profusion of peeling bark and wood chips. Running down the back side of the cavity in a jaggedly vertical line resembling a lightning bolt was a shaft of light, a split in the far side of the snag. The inner surface of the cavity, shadowed of course, mimicked the sunlit outer wood — variegated shades of muted browns and grays, pocked and stained by rain and sap, crossbarred by the tracks of wood-boring beetles and prospecting woodpeckers.

Something gnawed along the edges of my intuition. Something amiss. Something I could not consciously discern. Lightning bolts, in nature and in art, always end in a point. This one did not. This one was attenuated, ending abruptly, and though the front wall of the cavity, in full sunlight, was obviously several inches lower than the shadowed back wall, the shaft did not extend all the way down to the sunlight. Binoculared eyes returned to the shaft of light.

Starting at the top, dialing in the distance, working slowly downward... "Holy Jesus!" The explosion of realization and the accompanying surge of adrenaline began in the pit of my stomach and radiated outward to my extremities. I could feel individual hairs along my calves and on the backs of my hands. Its eyes were open, yellow pupils huge in the shadowed light. The jagged bolt had ended at the top of its shadowed head, though it was as if the

A clutch can contain as many as six eggs. The male feeds the incubating female during the latter days of the month-long incubation period. Because incubation begins with the first laid egg, the eggs hatch over sequential days and the young are noticeably different in size. They typically depart the nesting cavity in the order that they were hatched, at about one month of age.

Extremely nocturnal, these small owls catch mice that become active after dark and take small birds from night roosts. Insects, crayfish, and earthworms constitute much of their diet during the warmer months of the year.

bolt had continued on through me, this electrifying visual revelation making me unanticipated and uninvited privy to some sacred inner working of the natural world.

I dropped the binoculars and glanced at Scott. He knew that I knew. My eyes were as wide as the owl's. I looked back at the cavity. It was gone. I hadn't seen it leave. Deliberately, doggedly, I made myself calm down, slow down. I started again at the top, working down the shaft. No, wait! It was still there… or was it? Appearing, disappearing, appearing again, more a function of mindset than of visual acuity, so closely did the pattern of the bird's body feathers approximate the design of weathered, barkless wood.

Eastern Screech-Owl

IT IS EASY TO UNDERSTAND why, with its strange-sad, other-worldly vocalizations emanating from the dark forests, the Eastern Screech-Owl played large in Native American lore. For some tribes the screech owl was a harbinger of ill health or defeat in battle. For these and others a dream of the bird or a visit by the bird meant elaborate purifying rituals with the tribal shaman. Some knew the screech owl to be the agent of death, appearing as it did from the blackness of night, an escort for the soul as it were, from the light into the darkness.

Jim!

Years spent listening told me in an instant. The tone had changed abruptly, dramatically. The levity and the excitement, so recently and uncharacteristically recaptured, were inexorably gone, and all my mental programs came crashing down around us. In that instant I knew. My mother's call had not been about the owl. The owl was gone. No, wait! It was still there… waiting.

Jim, the oncologist called this morning. He says there's really nothing more they can do now.

Eastern Screech-Owl wing (red phase) from above and below.

Chapter Seven

Western Screech-Owl

The Western Screech-Owl is a small, nocturnal, woodland owl of western North America. It is one of the west's more common owls at lower elevations. Originally, this bird was called "Kennicott's Owl" to honor Robert Kennicott, an American explorer and naturalist. Other common names include Little Horned Owl, Dusk Owl, Ghost Owl, Mouse Owl, Cat Owl, and Puget Sound Screech Owl.

Blow-Up

CERTAINLY ONE component of the fascination with owls, by birders and non-birders alike, is the awareness that owls are at the top of the food chain. The fact that owls, for the most part, prey, kill, and eat in total darkness or along the shadowy edges of crepuscular light, rather than detracting from the mystique, seems only to enhance it. There is some atavistic pleasure taken by the ultimate predator upon seeing wolves, bears, falcons, and other charismatic predatory animals follow their instincts in broad day-light under the watchful eye of the hiker, naturalist, or the wildlife photographer's lens.

Add the element of impending nightfall or night itself and we have nuanced into a whole other emotional and psychological dimension where mystery and uncertainty reign. Wolves on a deer carcass, though not for the squeamish, is scrutable. It is clean. It is final. An owl in nightdark woods, rodent carcass secured to branch by daggered talon, is inscrutable. It is opaque.

Western Screech-Owls are squat-looking as they sit erect with their plumage fluffed out. They can appear not to have ear tufts if they are not raised, although the ear tufts are quite prominent when erect.

It raises questions. And we hesitate to venture about in night-dark woods looking for the answers.

Blood at the top of the food chain stirs us in ways that are both difficult and embarrassing to verbalize. Bones along the trail put the wild back in wildlife, with exclamatory punctuation. There is genetic coding deep within each of us that still remembers when. Each of us, at some elemental level, would rather stalk some distant ridge, atlatl in hand, than push a grocery cart through supermarket aisles congested with our own kind.

I have a good friend, mid-fifties, in perfect health and in possession of long-lived genes, who has made pacts and provisions with his family in case of the onset of a terminal illness. They are to transport him, while he is still ambulatory, to a riparian gorge running through high desert a day distant from any population center. He will disembark, water and sandwiches in pack, and disappear into canyon country news.

My friend is not a birdwatcher, but he is an owl enthusiast, despite having seen only one of the nineteen North American species and heard one other. By his descriptions I have deduced his sighted owl was a Great Horned and his heard owl was a Western Screech — the "tiger of the night" and the "little tiger of the night." Both were in his canyon of choice. Both added weight to his final decision.

The tiger of the night had come to him in the middle of the day, swooping in on a dead mouse which he had found and attached to a packstrap. He had rounded a bend in the streambed, flushed the owl, tossed the carcass toward it in a random moment of inspiration, then watched in awe as the Great Horned came in, totally oblivious to his presence.

Western Screech-Owl

The little tiger of the night had come to him in the middle of the night, awakening him at his trailhead campsite, keeping him awake with its incessant, high-pitched hollow hooting, accelerating into spooky tremolo. Chagrined that he had been unable to shine and see it, he was fascinated to learn of the Western Screech-Owl's generalization of prey considering its small size, ecstatic that such a fearsome little predator inhabited his beloved canyon, and absolutely jubilant to know it shied from nothing in that canyon save the tiger of the night. Dan's atavistic genes run shallower than most.

WHEN WE MOVED to Arizona in the fall of 1978 we had neither seen a Western Screech-Owl, nor had I photographed well any of the North American owls. Birding friends apprised us that Western Screeches were common-to-abundant in the deserts surrounding Phoenix, and even inhabited green areas within the city itself. They also assured us that this owl would respond to tape and was so ubiquitous in proper habitat that taping would not be detrimental to the species. Because of this abundance and accessibility, we put Western Screech-Owl at the top of our priority list and decided we would even attempt to photograph it, despite having no prior experience with flash photography.

Our first outings in the desert were, as expected, replete with nervous jocularity regarding snakes and scorpions, so it was with much anticipation that we planned our first trip to call up this small owl that counts these most-avoided desert denizens among its preferred prey. We knew also that Western Screeches will take rodents, lizards, and birds up to the size of quail, as well as insects. If it moves, if it is smaller than itself or even larger but non-threatening, Western Screech-Owls will take it. In the presence of Great Horneds, Western Screeches are not atop the food chain, but they most assuredly live large as the next link down.

The Verde River runs out of the Tonto National Forest, through saguaro, ironwood, and mesquite, along the eastern boundary of the Phoenix metroplex. On February 15, 1979,

Western Screech-Owl
Otus kennicottii

Most frequently heard vocalization
Series of "Hoo" notes, accelerating toward the end and dropping in pitch, sometimes likened to a "bouncing ball" sound. Notes are a bit more distinct than Eastern.

Size
A small owl, 7"-9" long, with a 20" wingspan; they are approximately the size of a cardinal or robin.

Most notable physical features
• prominent ear tufts
• young birds may lack conspicuous ears
• light underparts with heavy streaking and weak barring
• dark gray bill, yellow eyes
• very subtle regional variations in size and color; small portion of Pacific population is brown; the rest are gray; there is no red phase

Seasonal movement
Non-migratory; permanent resident

Nest sites
Tree cavities and saguaro cactus cavities; will use nest boxes

Habits
Extremely nocturnal

Range/habitat
Western Screech-Owls are found throughout the coastal lowlands, open forests, deciduous river bottoms, and deserts of the western U.S., and northward through the coast ranges of Canada.

well after dark on a night bitterly cold by southwest desert standards, we called up our first Western Screech-Owl along the Verde. No sooner had our recorder dispatched the bouncing ball vocalization through the still desert air, than the answer came back to us from the direction of a huge saguaro fifty feet away.

Instantly the owl flew from darkness, through our light beam, and landed at eye level in a mesquite directly in front of us. Thirty feet! There was no question in the owl's mind that these two unpracticed idiots juggling flashlight, tape recorder, tripod, camera, telephoto lens, two pair of binoculars, and an off-camera flash, were not what it had heard calling. I managed two frames before it whisked away into the surrounding blackness.

We had seen ear tufts and yellow eyes. We had been vaguely aware of dark vertical streaking on the underparts. We had size and voice. Other than that, nothing. We would have been hard pressed to write up decent field notes on our observation. After we untangled the flash sync cord from our legs, the tripod legs, and the rabbitbrush, we stood there for an hour, shivering, whispering excitedly, half expecting the vanished wraith to reappear.

On the way home we debated whether or not this had been a satisfying owl encounter. Certainly daylight would have been better than nighttime, but how many people ever observe an owl by day? Certainly we had been close. How many ever get this close to an owl, day or night? Would we have traded this close yet fleeting encounter for a more distant, yet longer look with time for leisurely study? The bottom line, to which we returned time after time as we analyzed what we could/should have done differently, was the photographs. There would be proof. There would be mementos.

I fiRST BECAME INTRIGUED with photography when we saw the 1966 movie *Blow-Up*, Michelangelo Antonioni's take on traditional British society being overtaken by the decadence and hedonism of the 1960s. The lead character, portrayed by David Hemmings, is a commercial photographer who unknowingly witnesses and photographs a murder. The realization that something

Owlets leave the nest at 28 days of age, but the parents will continue to care for them for an additional five to six weeks.

is amiss drives him into his darkroom where his insouciance toward his life and profession is transformed into intense purpose as he prints successively bigger enlargements of a pastoral park scene. In the final blow-up, the gun and the body emerge, shockingly, suspected yet still unexpected, from the grain of the original photo. The photographer's life is changed forever.

Movie and video have never appealed to me. Rather, I have always been fascinated by the still frame, by distilling an event, an experience, a moment into single image, frozen and indelible, spare and timeless — one visual to carry off forever in the mind.

To capture the exact essence of the moment is the challenge in bird photography — stilling the hummingbird's wing, catching the water droplets from the fish in the osprey's talons. And if, in printing this exact essence, something unexpected,

Western Screech-Owl

something undiscerned is found… well, that only happened to David Hemmings' character. The real unexpected in bird photography is simply to capture the image, any image at all, so flighty and wary are the instincts of the subjects. And how would one capture the essence of a creature whose substance is shadow and darkness?

BUT I KNEW I HAD moved the shutter twice on this little tiger of the night, and in the naive optimism of my inexperience with nighttime photography, I knew just as surely that the owl would be there in the slide, exactly as it appeared in my mind's eye — close, sharp, perfectly exposed. Anything less would be a devastating disappointment, ruining the experience and leaving nothing to jog the memories — the hunter with no prey.

These little owls are sedentary with few movements occurring outside of the young dispersing to find their own territory. They live to be about 13 years of age.

Anything more? What more could there be than a perfect portrait of a fleeting creature of the night? Capture the essence, capture the prey. One day, midweek after our Western Screech-Owl caper, Deva unexpectedly picked me up after work. She had a wild grin on her face. She had been to the film lab. She had been in the darkroom. She had interesting information.

What had the owl been doing when we had so unceremoniously interrupted it? I had no idea. What do owls ever do. Sleep. Hunt. Eat. I was still coming down from my workday, wasn't yet dialed in to my private life, surely wasn't focused on the private lives of owls. What would I say if she told me there was red in the photos? Of course there was no red — there was certainly no red in the scene I carried in my mind. Damn It! We hadn't gotten the flash far enough away from the camera to prevent "red eye!" Damn, Damn, Damn! Just what we had feared — a Western Screech photo with diagnostic yellow eyes turned bright red by reflection of flash from eye back into lens.

Finally I tuned in. Why was I cursing in disappointment while this woman sat there grinning? She reached into the back seat and handed me a print — the print. A 16x20 of the owl, filling fully half the frame. Against the out-of-focus natural background, from the soft, muted grays of the owl's own background color with its protective streaking and stippling of lights and darks, three things virtually leapt from the print.

The huge yellow eyes boring through the soul — *"Who is responsible for this interruption!"*

The row of small daggers, talons resting atop the branch — *"Who dares be about in my night-dark domain!"*

The smear of blood, unmistakably red on the dark beak and surrounding gray bristles — *"This is my essence; this is my owlness."*

The photo I took of the Western Screech-Owl.

Chapter Eight
Barn Owl

The Barn Owl is North America's only member of the family Tytonidae (all other owls are from the Strigidae family), sometimes called the monkey-faced owl family. Unlike all other owls, it has a distinctive heart-shaped facial disk. It also has relatively long legs (the only other owl with long legs is the Burrowing Owl). It is found in virtually all habitats but much more abundantly in open woodland, prairies, and fields than forested country. They usually roost by day in tree hollows but have also been found in caves, wells, outbuildings, or thick foliage.

Poltergeist

BEHIND ME, TO THE SOUTH, a huge thunderhead was boiling up over the high shoulders of the Santa Ritas, presaging this evening's edition of the Arizona monsoon season. One hundred yards downslope, through a veritable garden of thorns devoid of anything tall enough to provide any shade, my van had just been enveloped by another dust devil. It was easily one hundred degrees, but this was not the dry heat of Arizona's wonderful winters. It was the stifling heat of early afternoon in Arizona's humid dog days of August. Sweating and swearing, both profusely, I watched with stinging fascination as the rivulets of perspiration dropping from my chin traced a miniature river through the patina of dust on my forearm and mingled with the blood from myriad scratches where I had waded through the catclaw — common name, "Wait-a Minute!"

The first of the three mineshafts had produced nothing. Fenced off with barbed wire and signed with warnings of danger, the shaft

Barn Owls specialize in hunting small ground mammals. They rely greatly on their silent flight and extremely acute hearing to locate prey. The sound of the Barn Owl's wings is muffled by a velvety pile on the feather surface. In addition, the leading edges of the wing feathers have a fringe or fine comb which deadens the sound of the wing beats.

was roughly square at the top, perhaps four feet by four feet and appeared to be fifteen feet deep with perpendicular sides and water in the bottom. Spider webs festooned the deeper, darker crevices and dead frogs and insects floated on the murky, dark water. Basically, this was the abandoned mineshaft of your worst nightmare.

How deep was the water? How rotten was the rock? How long could an unfortunate soul cling to life in those depths before the next dummy ventured up this desolate hill on this deserted forest service road to nowhere? I shuddered mentally, knowing that no sound emanating from the shaft would ever reach the road, knowing there was absolutely no reason for anyone to ever fight their way up that steep and thorny slope, knowing I had already experienced most of the several reasons not to.

Moving laterally twenty yards across the hillside, keeping the sun at my face so that my shadow would not precede me, I edged slowly and cautiously up to the barbed wire surrounding the second shaft. Nothing. Somewhat larger and more open at the top, it was not as apparently deep as the first shaft, but the bottom sloped down and out of sight under an overhanging ledge of crumbling dirt and rock. A different nightmare: depth unknown, dangers unsuspected. I shuddered again, physically this time.

The final opening was forty yards farther, higher, closer to the ridgeline, and bore no wire or warnings. Sidestepping the murderous points of a large Spanish dagger, I began picking my way up through the loose rubble and thorny scrub. My eyes were on the ground, but my mind was somewhere else, most likely on the futility of what I was doing here and how animated the conversation was going to be when I next saw the friend who had suggested this little excursion.

The *Hissssssing* caught me totally off guard, welled up as if exactly under my feet, shocked up the hackles along my spine, on up the back of my neck, then receded slightly but seemed still to fill the heavy, humid air on all sides of me. I cast about wildly on the ground for the snake, knowing full well that rattle means close, hissing means too close. And knowing in that split second between realization and the certain strike that I had let physical discomfort and my disappointment interdict a proper awareness of my surroundings.

But… there was no snake. In the split second after this second realization, I came to a third — my search had been successful. I had a wry laugh at my little snakedance there on the hillside. I promised an apology to my friend. I got down on my belly and slithered to the lip of the third shaft. Peering into the shadowed depths, I saw six fluid, dark eyes peering back up at me. There were two dirty white fuzzballs that in about six weeks would be fledgling Barn Owls, and there was a parent with them, presumably the female.

This shaft was shallower than the first two, but still deep and steep enough to beg the question why it too had not been enclosed and signed. The nest, simply a scrape in the dirt detritus, was on a ledge, elevated several inches above

Barn Owl
Tyto alba

Most frequently heard vocalization
Long, shrill, raspy, hissing shriek; common year round

Size
A medium-sized owl, 16" long, with a 42" wingspan; they are approximately the size of a crow.

Most notable physical features
• round-headed without ear tufts
• very pale body color
• distinctive white heart-shaped facial disk; dark eyes
• long-legged
• broad but fairly pointed wings
• distinguished in flight by its large head

Seasonal movement
Permanent resident with some withdrawal from northern range in winter

Nest sites
Tree cavities, barns, cliff cavities, abandoned mine shafts

Habits
Nocturnal

Range/habitat
Barn Owls are found in open country, fields, farmlands, marshes, groves, barns, towns, and cliffs throughout the continental U.S., except for the northern plains and the Rocky Mountains.

Barn Owls will breed any time during the year, depending on food supply. The majority of Barn Owls nest in tree hollows up to 60 feet high, but they will also nest in old buildings, caves, and well shafts.

the shaft's floor, on the west wall. It appeared that the female, in the infinite wisdom of her instincts, had laid the eggs in the only place where neither accumulated rain water nor intense summer sun would ever touch them. Now the little fuzzballs, showing off just a few lines of brown above their eyes at the top of their already-formed facial disks, had something on which to practice their spooky vocals. The hissing never abated until I had pulled back from the opening and begun my retreat down the hill. Presumably, since Barn Owls seem to be strictly nocturnal hunters, this was not a contact call to the second adult on a rodent run, but simply an alarm/warning call. I had been both alarmed and warned. It was my first encounter with Barn Owl young, but it was not my first experience with Barn Owl vocalizations.

Hiss, wonderfully onomatopoeic as it is, is only the second most frequently-used word to describe the barn owl's wide vocal repertoire. "Shriek" seems more popular, and describes well the most frequently-heard offering. I had been witness to Barn Owl shrieking three times — three times that I would like to forget.

The first occurred in Bentsen State Park in Texas. The previous evening I had talked with another camper around his campfire about his probable mountain lion sighting earlier in the week. Cougar sound is often described as a woman screaming. On this trip I was using a small backpack tent, tapered to allow just enough height at the foot of the tent to dress oneself on one's knees. In pre-dawn darkness I was awakened to terrible shrieks

Barn Owl

just above my head. I sat bolt upright in my bag, then heaved myself to my feet — at the head of the tent. Needless to say, by the time I got the debacle of zippers, stakes, guyropes, and tentfly straightened out in the dark, the vocalist was long gone. Morning light revealed a perfect owlsnag, with the requisite whitewash, just over the head of the tent. Cougar or Barn Owl, whichever, probably died laughing somewhere in the Texas bush.

Y NEXT TWO encounters with Barn Owls shrieking mirrored perfectly all the literary references to these owls down through history — whenever man has heard Barn Owls at night, something weird or something bad (usually both) is in the offing. Both incidents occurred in low desert southwest of Phoenix, an area that extensive irrigation has made extremely suitable for agriculture, primarily cotton. Cotton culture may be the bane of

The Barn Owl's ear openings are at slightly different levels on the head, and set at different angles. They are covered by a flexible ruff made up of short, densely-webbed feathers that frame the face, turning it into a dish-like reflector for sound. This gives the Barn Owl very sensitive and directional hearing, with which it can locate prey even in total darkness.

Barn Owl

southwestern environmentalists for what it does to the water table, but it has provided an ideal habitat for barn owls.

Gila Bend, Arizona, often records the hottest temperatures in the nation in summer. In August of 1993, the summer monsoons caused extensive flooding along the Gila River and state listers were making weekly treks to scope for rare shorebirds on the newly-created mudflats. One weekend, having joined this search and having decided to camp over, I realized it was too hot and steamy to sleep inside my van and threw my sleeping bag on top of the van as a cooler option. I dozed fitfully, not realizing area farmers had their aerial spraying done at night to take advantage of windless conditions.

I am unsure whether the plane spooked the Barn Owl, which then flushed over and awakened me, or if a flyover owl spooked me awake to the oncoming drone of the plane. You can be sure that owlshriek and the hum of the propeller cluttered my sleepy brain with enough stimuli to make me totally forget I was atop my van rather than in it. I have never told this story to anyone. I will not reveal the extent of my injuries. I sustained no permanent brain damage. Owl and pilot are probably still laughing.

Opposite: The Barn Owl calls infrequently, but its usual call is a drawn-out rasping screech. When surprised in its roosting hollow or nest, it makes hissing and rasping noises. Above: Although it will pounce on prey from a perch, it normally flies low (less than 10 feet from the ground) and dives onto prey with talons extended. Although the Barn Owl is highly nocturnal, it can be observed hunting in daylight.

The Barn Owl's favorite habitat consists of open, low-lying areas, preferably below 750 feet elevation, with an abundant vole population. Although the owl has an extensive range, it is uncommon higher in the mountains, and they avoid areas with low winter temperatures, dense forests, and intensive cultivation.

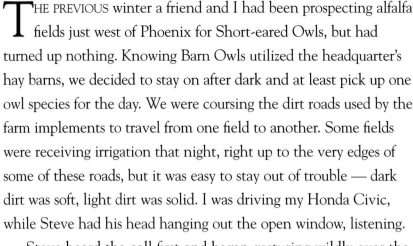

THE PREVIOUS winter a friend and I had been prospecting alfalfa fields just west of Phoenix for Short-eared Owls, but had turned up nothing. Knowing Barn Owls utilized the headquarter's hay barns, we decided to stay on after dark and at least pick up one owl species for the day. We were coursing the dirt roads used by the farm implements to travel from one field to another. Some fields were receiving irrigation that night, right up to the very edges of some of these roads, but it was easy to stay out of trouble — dark dirt was soft, light dirt was solid. I was driving my Honda Civic, while Steve had his head hanging out the open window, listening.

Steve heard the call first and began gesturing wildly over the top of the car. I stuck my head out the window, peering intently at the night sky. The owl went right over us, shrieking. No… of course that's not right. The owl was laughing. I hadn't come to a complete stop and my steering hand drifted as I followed the owl with my head. I buried us in mud up to the hubs. Three hours later, covered with mud, dirt still glupping and glopping under the fenders, we drove out past the main silo. The Barn Owl was up there, laughing down at us.

THE BARN OWL may well have been Lady MacBeth's "fatal bellman," notorious as it was in the Old World as an inhabitant of church belfries. But nothing demythologizes like proximity and utility. As the human population of the New World grew up around the cave- and tree cavity-inhabiting Barn Owl, the owls adapted, making a living in and off man's structures and agricultural practices. And being more widespread throughout the continent south of Canada than other owls, and given their preference for mice and rats, Barn Owls have been recognized, albeit later rather than sooner, as the most beneficial to man of all the owls

In the East, barn owls have benefited greatly from nestbox programs. In the West, it seems not a stretch to say that most barns, both operational and abandoned, either have a resident Barn Owl or are on one's nightly route. Like their brethren, the burrowing owls, they are now urbanites as well. We have seen them in residential palm groves, in city dumps, and in shelterbelts along park concourses. And in twenty-five years of recording Barn Owl sightings, our most numerous records have come from freeway bridge abutments! Along with golf course Burrowing Owls, this now makes possible another positive tick for man's environmental disregard here in the Southwest.

Indeed, though they are not often seen, Barn Owls are so common in and around man that most serious birders do not go out looking for them. Most have had their requisite handful of interesting, usually unexpected Barn Owl sightings and have honed their Barn Owl weird stories.

I am not looking for Barn Owls anymore either. But, like some horror movie aficionado deliciously anticipating the next body in the closet, I anxiously await my next encounter, totally unsuspected as I know it must be. Let's just hope, when the shrieking and the laughter break out, that I'm not doing anything at which I can seriously injure myself.

Barn Owl wing from above and below.

Chapter Nine
Elf Owl

The Elf Owl is the smallest owl in the world. Its small size, desert habitat, and nocturnal nature make it easily distinguished from any other owl. It is a highly-migratory owl, completely leaving the United States for Mexico in winter. When danger approaches, an Elf Owl straightens its body, covers its lighter underparts with one wing, then turns its head and peers over the bent wing with the top of its eyes. They are not very aggressive, preferring to fly away rather than fight.

Harbinger

I HAVEN'T BEEN ABLE to listen to country/western music since the spring of 1995. I have assiduously avoided C&W on the airwaves, at concert venues, even in the pages of the Sunday entertainment supplement. I'd like to chronicle the cause as my cheatin' wife, my dyin' dog, and the mournful whistle of an outbound freight silhouetted on the slow settin' sun. Actually, it was the mournful whistle of an Elf Owl drifting through the moonlit silhouettes of cactus and mesquite at a lonesome campground deep in the Texas outback. I think that sentence you just read certainly contains enough C&W cliches to compensate for the seemingly discordant element of the owl. It happened like this…

The concrete of U.S. 385 tracks across the tans and beiges in the vast emptiness of the Chihuahuan Desert of West Texas like white scar tissue. Scorpions hold their national conventions here, and rainclouds come here to die. There is little vegetation. There is even less water. There is no radar.

Opposite: Although Elf Owls are abundant in saguaro deserts, they are also quite abundant into the mountains reaching elevations of up to about 6,000 feet. They can be found in dense mesquite, dry oak woodlands, wooded canyons, and sycamores.

This morning in the spring of 1995 found me heading north out of Big Bend for Marathon. My speedometer needle had just kissed 100 when a band of malpais buzzards swept over the road. Bringing up the rear was a bird so low that I could count the three white tail bands even at that speed — a female Zonie, a Zone-tailed Hawk. I punched the rental's radio button. If thorn scrub, vultures, and country/western stations weren't invented in West Texas, then surely they have reached their zenith there — John Berry was singing *Standing On The Edge Of Goodbye.*

Tears welled up instantly, overflowed into steady rivulets on the steering wheel, and I broke down sobbing — not a cool thing at 100 miles per hour. I had come to the park for a few days of solitude, to see if a few days away from reality would help me step back, away from that edge John Berry was singing about. He was dealing with good love gone bad. I was dealing with the imminent loss of my mother's three year battle with breast cancer. I wrestled the car onto the road shoulder, bailed, and ran crying into the desert

IT ALL CAME FLOODING back: three years ago, the diagnosis; a year ago, astonishingly enough on the morning after a screech owl had wailed on her bedroom windowsill all night, her oncologist had phoned to utter the most terrifyingly irrevocable word in our language — terminal. In a birding lifetime of searching for owlsign, both physically in the wilds and intellectually in literature, I had never once given any personal credence to all the well-documented instances of primitive man's owlfear. I had that morning.

Trying, as I always had, to allay life's realities with a little birding, I had come to Big Bend ostensibly to hike for the Colima Warbler and to grapple with decisions regarding the settlement of my mother's affairs. But in the heart of my heart I knew I was looking for a sign. Standing on the precipice of our species' deepest abyss, I still wanted to know why, I still needed to address my denial, I still hoped to avert that final step over that dread edge. An Elf Owl had come to me in the night, in startling coincidence, just as the screech owl had come to my mother. Owl-sign. Unsought. Unsolicited.

No one comes to Big Bend for Elf Owl. Most birders come to Big Bend for the Colima Warbler. Some come for Lucifer Hummingbird or Zone-tailed Hawk. Elf Owls are much easier and more common in southern Arizona. They are often chanced upon in the lower Rio Grande Valley. I certainly had not come here looking for one. Elf sightings constitute my second longest Arizona owl list, less numerous only than Great Horned, and we had spent many sleepless nights there either looking for this tiny owl or wishing it would take its marvelous little high-pitched, accelerating, six-syllable bark someplace else so that we could sleep.

On the afternoon of my arrival I had hiked from the Basin campground into Boot Springs via Laguna Meadow, in ninety degree temperatures, in three hours. My quart of water disappeared quickly. I heard several Colimas but saw none of them well. I still knew my mother's indomitable will to live would pull her through.

That night one of West Texas' notorious April Blue Northers blew through the mostly-deserted campground. Except for my weight pinning it to the desert floor, my tent would have been long flown. I awoke to grit in my teeth and leaves drifted around my sleeping bag, quickly realizing the need for stocking cap and gloves. I hiked into Boot Springs via Laguna Meadow in less than an hour, trying to warm up. I never touched my water. I saw several Colimas well and photographed one. I still knew my mother's unwavering religious faith would pull her through.

Elf Owl
Micrathene whitneyi

Most frequently heard vocalization
Repeated series of fairly sharp, high-pitched, rapid barking notes, falling off at the end

Size
Our smallest owl, 5.5" long, with a 13" wingspan; approximately the size of a sparrow.

Most notable physical features
- tiny, slim size with a relatively small head; no ear tufts
- finely speckled gray overall
- buffy underparts with indistinct streaking
- short tail separates it from Northern and Ferruginous Pygmy-Owls

Seasonal movement
Highly migratory; leaves the U.S. in winter

Nest sites
Woodpecker holes in saguaro cactus, sycamore and oak trees, and occasionally in utility poles

Habits
Nocturnal; roosts by day in holes in giant cactus

Range/habitat
Southern Arizona, southwestern New Mexico, and southwestern Texas; their habitat is saguaro deserts and riparian canyons in mountain foothills.

The owl came to me that night, as in a dream, shortly after I had crawled stone-toed cold into my bag. Tossing and turning, I finally awoke drenched with sweat — at 5,500 feet in the Chisos Mountains the first night after a cold front's passage! I listened breathlessly, fully recalling Apache legends that told of owl-dreams signifying approaching death. The Chisos were deep within Apache territory. The Elf Owl had been deep within the realm of Apache folklore. The calling began anew. I exhaled. At least this was no dream. And the owl was very close.

On a whim I grabbed the flashlight and wriggled out of the tent. On one owling excursion into Guadalupe Canyon on Arizona's New Mexico border, eight of us wielding five flashlights had tried unavailingly for an hour to shine a continuously calling Elf Owl in a mesquite right before us. Vengeful perhaps, it had then kept us awake all night. This is a sparrow-sized owl, and the mesquite thicket behind the campsite was dense. I had little hope of seeing this owl nor any rational reason for wanting to. But even cursory review of tribal folktales reminds us that owls and reason bear no correlation, unless it is an inverse one.

I pointed the light toward the largest mesquite and flicked the switch. Remarkably, against all logic of past experience, the owl appeared right there, centered in the beam, so close it seemed I could reach out and touch it. Huge yellow eyes never leaving me, it sat very calm and still, quite at odds with the usually frenetic little birds of my Arizona Elf Owl experience, which flitted nervously from branch to branch, from branch to cactus hole and back out again. The bright white eyebrows arched upward lending every appearance that I would summarily be reprimanded, or at least interrogated.

What are you doing here in my park?

Instinctively, my head swiveled and I glanced about, though I knew as I did it, there was no one there save the Elf and me. The lightbeam swung back. He was still there. Unmoving. Unmoved. Rubbing my eyes, in a voice that was but a hoarse croak betraying equal parts astonishment and embarrassment, I mentioned my

Opposite: Elf Owls nest exclusively in woodpecker holes found in saguaro cacti, sycamores, pines, walnuts, and even telephone poles.

Elf Owl

The Elf Owl's diet consists mainly of spiders, insects, and scorpions. They will also eat beetles, moths, grasshoppers, and crickets. Most prey is captured in flight.

mother, explained I was looking for a sign, asked why he would not let me sleep.

I am an agent of the darkness. The night is my realm.

Yes, I was well aware of that, having first seen him in an old cemetery grove in Tubac, well past midnight, an early migrant in the second week of March. But I had also seen him in lighttime. Once in Ramsey, ╪harassed by titmice. And one Easter morning fleeing down Madera from the cacophony of the boom boxes. And I had heard him in Chino, calling at mid-day from deep within a Saguaro. Was he the sign?

Look to the eastern sky. There's a bad moon rising.

I looked. The night was cloudless. A luminous glow was beginning to suffuse the peaks around Pinnacle Pass. Wryly I wondered to myself, for I was afraid he might take umbrage at this mockery, if he was into rock & roll, a CCR fan. Aloud, I asked him if this was about my mother.

An escort has already been dispatched for your mother.

This brought me up short on two accounts. Instantly regretting my momentary mindslip into sarcasm, for who could cipher whether this wraith could read minds, I was overcome anew with sadness for my mother's condition and terrified by another thought. No matter how the survivors delude themselves, the grief is still in large measure about their own mortality. Is this about me?

Get your things together. Tend to your lists.

I AWOKE TO SUNLIGHT and birdsong. The sleeping bag was twisted and wadded beneath me, and I struggled to extricate myself, unrefreshed and feeling stiff and sore from the up-canyon hikes on the preceding days. I sat at a breakfast of cold cereal and hot tea, pen in hand, writing in my notebook: priest; florist; estate sales; bank accounts; gravestone… Finishing the list and setting about to chronologize it, my mind kept wandering off to some unnamed task, some unresolved issue.

Returning to the notebook to see what I had forgotten, I glanced toward the mesquites at the foot of the tent. Immediately I was overcome with that ominous feeling that accompanies the sudden recognition of something that has to be done even though the outcome is probably to be dreaded.

I walked to the nearest mesquite and dropped to my knees beneath the largest horizontal branch. A small portion of my brain suggested formulating a prayer and leaving, but I dropped to the task, carefully brushing aside leaves and picking though the natural detritus. They were there! I leaped up and thrust an index finger toward the gibbous moon fading fast along the western sky.

There were two of them. Using a knife and a small stick, I carefully pulled them apart in the bowl of my breakfast spoon— grasshopper wings, the fragmented black shell of some hapless beetle, two tiny, horny talons that could only be lizard's toes, and near the elf's regurgitated pellets, but not in them, I found two thin, hardened, thread-like wands, perhaps scorpion stingers — a literal sorcerer's brew that some ancient tribesman might have concocted to ease some mysterious malady — or to induce a dream in which the sorcerer himself might have appeared and spoken.

Breaking camp quickly, I loaded the car, left the park, and buried my foot in the accelerator. I knew I had gained some modicum of closure, and I was anxious to leave before being overcome by the urge to seek out the owl's daytime roost, before being overcome by the urge to seek hard answers to half articulated questions posed by the previous night's… events.

Halfway to Marathon the buzzards had crossed my path, I had punched up John Berry, and I had run crying into the desert. Sitting on a rock, out of sound and sight of the scar tissue that is I-385, I composed myself by writing the principle facts in my notebook. I wrote down four things: I was alive; my

Elf Owls often hover over insect prey, which causes the insects to take flight, then capture them in mid air. They also pluck insects from tree branches or the ground without taking off, and forage by walking on the ground.

Elf Owl

mother was dying; I found C&W song themes too sad and downbeat for my personal taste; I had seen an Elf Owl last night at my campsite.

On the next page I wrote down four corollary facts: I would be alive tomorrow if I slowed down and drove in a rational manner; my mother might be dead tomorrow, but I had known for many years that this day in our relationship would arrive; I would never again listen to country/western music; despite literary efforts to the contrary from authors as disparate in time and intention as Chaucer to Tony Hillerman, owls did not foretell human affairs.

I dried my eyes. I returned to the car. I pulled back onto the scar tissue of I-385. I punched up the radio once again. It was another C&W station — no surprise there. As I reached to hit the search and seek button — there must be a rock station in West Texas — the song was interrupted for a news bulletin. Now there was a surprise, as I hadn't been sure that C&W stations acknowledged hard news.

This was hard news. It was April 19th. The capitol of Oklahoma had just become an icon, a stand-alone sentence. Oklahoma City. I would never again look for elf owls either.

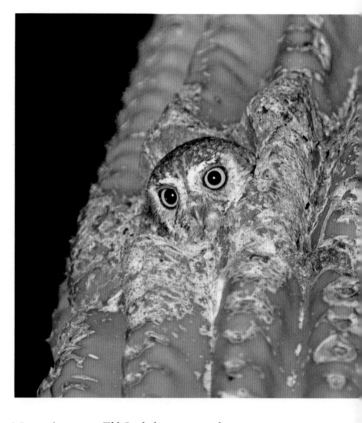

Elf Owls have many distinct vocalizations. The primary call of the male is a high-pitched yip, "whi-whi-whi-whi-whi." Five to 20 notes are given during each sequence, and calling can be almost continuous through the night. Calling is most intense during early evening and near dawn on moonlit spring nights.

Chapter Ten

Northern Saw-whet Owl

The Northern Saw-whet Owl is known for being quite tame and approachable in the daytime where it will often perch quite low (as low as five feet off the ground). This small owl lacks ear tufts, and has a proportionately large head and prominent facial disk. The Saw-whet Owl's name comes from the "skiew" call that is made when it is alarmed. This sound resembles the whetting of a saw.

Brain Food

DEVA AND I WERE DRIVING ACROSS northern Wisconsin, coming from an appointment with Kirtland's Warbler. We had arranged a meeting with Yellow Rail at McGregor Marsh for the following evening. With a little time to kill, we called a local hotline looking for information on Connecticut Warblers and picked up the name of Larry Semo who was doing bird research in the area that summer. Larry told us to meet him at his field station in the woods the next morning. He couldn't promise the warbler, but he did have something to show us he thought we might find interesting.

It proved very interesting. As Larry handed it to Deva I watched the expression on her face change subtly from wonder and delight, to wonder and hesitancy, to wonder and anxiety. One week from fledging, the baby Northern Saw-whet Owl, not even a handful, was instinctively tightening down on her finger with both little talons. It drew no blood, but marks were still apparent the following day.

                                    Northern Saw-whet Owl

Northern Saw-whet Owls inhabit coniferous and deciduous forests, with thickets of second-growth or shrubs. They occur mainly in forests with deciduous trees, where woodpeckers create cavities for nest sites. Breeding habitat is usually swampy or wet rather than dry.

This little saw-whet was one of a pair of siblings hatched out of a nesting box Larry had put up in the spring. This one seemed passive and shy, but the one Larry held was very alert and trying out its wings amidst much bill clacking. They were old enough now, though not quite yet able to fly, that the parents were coming to the nest only at night. We had seen only one Northern Saw-whet prior to this, also an immature — a face only, appearing high above us in a flicker hole in the Chiricahuas of Arizona. Though Saw-whets' tameness was legendary, "in hand" it surprised us almost as much as the bright rufous tones on the juvenile underparts.

FOUR SUMMERS LATER, August found us setting up camp outside the Ruby Mountain Wilderness of northeast Nevada, on our way to a rendezvous with Himalayan Snowcock. As I pounded the last tent stake, a robin flashed by, brilliant in the setting sun, and disappeared into a large Ponderosa next to the campsite. Minutes later, returning with the ice chest, I glanced up to a low horizontal branch overhanging the picnic table. Robin indeed, five feet away from my face an immature saw-whet was studying me impassively.

Deva was topless, washing her long hair in the privacy of the open side-doors of our van. Heeding my exclamation, she immediately came running, as was, to the table, slinging water everywhere. Such is the awe quotient of the owl that I never gave her a glance. Such is the awe quotient of the owl that on two long-planned and carefully-itineraried trips to successfully add such coveted birds as Kirtland's Warbler, Yellow Rail, Connecticut Warbler, and Himalayan Snowcock to our lifelist, Saw-whet Owl, though not a life bird, was overwhelmingly voted "bird of the trip" on both occasions.

Eastern birders may not understand this saw-whet excitement. They seem to encounter this little owl, the smallest of their owls, far more often and easily than their western counterparts. It may be that saw-whets are more common in the east. Larry Semo told us saw-whets were by far the most common breeding owl in the Great Lakes states, with literally hundreds passing through the banding stations at Woodland Dunes and Whitefish Point every migration season.

Another explanation is that in the west saw-whets are high mountain breeders. Winter saw-whet movement there is a vertical one, which spreads them out and disperses them, compared to the latitudinal movement in the east, which concentrates them in areas long-since discovered and well known to eastern owlers.

Our Nevada saw-whet was content to grace us with its presence while we slowly and quietly spread dinner in the dying light and ate in rapt attention, never imagining our crepuscular visitor was about to return the invitation. For twenty minutes it sat still and unmoving until finally some lower threshold of light triggered some higher threshold of owlness.

Most frequently heard vocalization
Series of "Hoo" notes, mellow, low, mechanical, and repeated endlessly (often 100-300 times per minute); very similar to Northern Pygmy-Owl but with regular rhythm.

Size
A small owl, 8" long with a 17" wingspan; similar to the Boreal Owl, but smaller with shorter tail; smaller than screech-owls, with longer wings.

Most notable physical features
• large head and triangular white face patch give wide-eyed, inquisitive look
• body has reddish tones
• underparts blotchy brown streaks
• yellow eyes
• juvenile has distinctive bright buffy underparts

Seasonal movement
Migratory; withdraws from Northern parts of range in winter

Nest sites
Woodpecker and natural tree cavities; will use nest boxes

Habits
Nocturnal

Range/habitat
Southeastern Alaska, Canada, the northern tier of the lower 48 states, and the mountain west; dense conifer forests and tamarack bogs

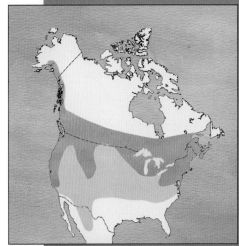

Yellow eyes became more alert, tracking sights we could not see. Round, tuftless head became more mobile, following sounds we could not hear. Small chunky body began to twitch and quiver, answering rhythms we could not fathom. Suddenly, startlingly for we were totally mesmerized, it swept down past us and pounced, near a stump not ten yards from our table.

One tiny squeak. A brief commotion. Then a moment of stillness in which the owl looked up, swaying slowly as those tiny daggered talons dug and tightened. Sitting there in stunned silence on the threshold of darkness we watched as the owl mantled its prey and began to eat. I glanced at Deva. Subconsciously, for I asked her about it the next day, she had taken her owl finger in her other hand and was rubbing it gently, absently.

Banders in the midwest have often taken from their nets Northern Saw-whets with decapitated songbirds in their clutches. Morning light revealed the body of a vole at the stump, headless. We know that some Native American tribes ate the internal organs of esteemed rivals, hoping to assume the fallen warrior's courage or strength. Could this concept be the basis of many tribes' reverence for the owl as the icon of wisdom?

IT WAS THE FOLLOWING winter that I saw my first adult Northern Saw-whet. A keen-eyed park employee had found the owl, a winter rarity for Arizona's low deserts, roosting in citrus trees at a state park, and provided state listers with an eastern saw-whet moment.

In the group arriving as the park opened on the third day after discovery were a handful of the most travelled, studied, and observant birders in Arizona. We all headed directly to the citrus grove, searched diligently there, then spread out up and down the trail and through a small tamarisk grove to a perennial stream running through a lowland section of the park, probably a dozen people total combing an area of two acres.

We combed for two hours, without success. A few left, leaving the rest of us mumbling and grumbling. I bushwhacked one

Juvenile Saw-whet Owls are tan to light reddish-brown on the undersides. The darker brown upper chest and head make it appear as if it is wearing a dark brown hood. A bold, white "V" above the bill and into the eyebrows is distinctive.

more time to the stream, found nothing, and on the way back to the path caught my bootlace on a low branch. Stopping in front of a small tamarisk out in the open that I had scrutinized carefully several times, I bent to retie. As I stood up I glanced one more time into the depths of the tree. The owl was right there, next to the bole, at eye level, staring at me from five feet, the coarse, stringy green tendrils that pass for leaves on a tamarisk effectively obliterating its owlshape.

Each and every one of the eight remaining searchers avowed to have looked into this tree at least twice and walked all the way around it each time. The owl had not moved that morning. Indeed it did not move the rest of the day up to the time the park closed in late afternoon. Such was the perfect protective camouflage of this bird in this tree that some reported going for lunch, returning to the tree unable to find it, returning yet again later still only to rediscover it and realize it had been there all along!

THE SHORTER THE LIST, the more special the listings, a concept longtime birders understand very well. To date we have only five records of Northern Saw-whet, the third smallest total of any species in our owl log. We have never attempted to tape this species. To my knowledge, we have never even heard it vocalize. But we have held no other owl species in our hands, alive. We have seen only one other owl species make a kill. We have seen only three others with a kill. Thus, the richness of our saw-whet experiences exceeds that of all the other owl species.

Davis and Russell, authors of *Finding Birds in Southeastern Arizona*, call Northern Saw-whet a "rare and rather irregular resident of mixed conifer forest at highest elevations," an opinion which paraphrases *The Birds of Arizona*, Phillips, Monson, and Marshall's seminal work. Recently, however, there have been breeding season reports of saw-whets in juniper/oak associations lower in the mountains. Perhaps they are at home in lower elevations than previously suspected. Perhaps they are more plentiful than previously suspected.

The Northern Saw-whet Owl lacks ear tufts, but has a relatively large head. This nocturnal owl is about the size of a Baltimore Oriole.

Undeterred by these reports, we have decided we will not actively seek this owl. More so than the rarer, more northerly species of owl-search legend, Northern Saw-whet seems to have become our defining owl — elusive, aloof, there when least expected, there only when unsought. Even as I looked up, disbelieving, into the face of the saw-whet in the tamarisk, amazed that I had found it, I had the eerie knowledge that this owl had found me. Or perhaps this owl deigned that I should see where others had not seen.

In the week following the tamarisk sighting I had three fragmented, separate but interwoven dreams:

The Saw-whet's diet consists mainly of woodland mice, with voles being favored second. This small owl has also been reported to take mammals as large as flying squirrels and birds as large as Rock Doves and Northern Cardinals. It has very good night vision and exceptional hearing.

I was very old and very gray. I was hiking in mountains up long, steep trails, vaguely familiar. My world had irrevocably changed, loved ones having all preceded me. It was summertime but the threat of winter hung imminently from my stooped shoulders. I was immensely unhappy, immensely desperate, immensely resolute in the knowledge of what I was going to do, what I must do. Falling exhausted before a grotto with a waterfall, I rested and waited. Downtrail flew an owl. It was a saw-whet. It landed on my outstretched hand. I peered into its wise, all-knowing eyes and acknowledged my readiness, my assent,

Northern Saw-whet Owl

and, as I did so, the bird expired. Using the leatherman's tool from my keyring, with deft hands I cleaned the feathers from the owl's head and bored a small hole through the top of its skull. A final shaft of light from the slowly setting sun sliced through the trees. Cupping the bird to my face, I pressed my lips against the hole. As the warm, congealed fluid filled my mouth, the last sunshaft strobed from behind an overhanging bough, enveloping the grotto. Blinded by the light, I felt myself slipping through the hole, into a vortex, spiraling downward...

Desperately, foolishly, I fought the awakening, trying consciously to will this scene to culmination. Priests and poets through the eons have both feared and revered the owl — herald of death, repository of wisdom. They knew this was no anomaly. They knew there was no dichotomy. There will be one more saw-whet for me, attendant at the end.

Northern Saw-whet Owl wing from above and below.

Chapter Eleven
Burrowing Owl

The Burrowing Owl is the only owl in North America that lives in a hole in the ground. It can often be found sitting at the entrance of its burrow in the daytime, although it is mainly crepuscular or nocturnal. The burrows are generally vacated rodent holes as the owl does not typically dig its own. The Burrowing Owl is readily distinguished by its long legs, as none of the other small owls have distinctive long legs.

Entry-Level Awesome

JP WAS fiVE, VERY talkative but very mellow. Devin was six, very inquisitive and… well, no one had ever accused Devin of being mellow. They were sitting on my lap, actually one on each knee, at rapt attention to the scene unfolding not ten yards below us at the bottom of this small rise. Never had I seen JP go this long without talking. Never had I seen Devin go this long without moving. At our backs the June Arizona sun was a setting fireball. At our feet, or practically so, two fledgling Burrowing Owls, parent-sized but still sprouting fuzzy down atop their heads, were returning the bumbles' rapt inquisitivity from in front of their "burrow."

The "bumbles," JP and Devin, were fourth generation birders, novice birders and initiate owlers in a family who had always put owling above cleanliness and punctuality. These fledglings were their "life" owls. By all appearances from their vertical postures, their gawky rubbernecking, and their wide-eyed return stares,

Burrowing Owls have been reported to nest in loose colonies. Such groupings may be a response to a local abundance of burrows and food, or an adaptation for mutual defense. Colony members can alert each other to the approach of predators and join in driving them off.

these fledglings had never seen birders before either. But we knew they had seen a lot of people, mostly people who kept walking and didn't stop to stare. People with clubs!

IT IS A MEASURE of the owl tribes' diversity and adaptability that non-birding outdoorspeople who have never seen an owl but realize they are out there, always seem taken aback and perhaps a little disappointed to see burrowing owls not "out there," but right here, as part of a viable cityscape. The bumbles and I were "right here" on the banks of Indian Bend Wash, a ten-mile long, up to half-mile wide floodplain, cutting a green and brown gash through the heart of this bustling suburban city at the edge of the country's fifth largest metropolitan area.

In times past, in the West and Southwest, prairie dog towns provided Burrowing Owls with their favored habitat. With the extirpation of the dogtowns at the behest of cattlemen, Burrowing Owl populations have undergone perhaps the greatest decline of all the owls, despite the more publicized travails of such species as the Spotted and Barn. Indian Bend Wash, better known as the Scottsdale Greenbelt, reads like a checklist of all the human development which has inadvertently provided breeding habitat for Burrowing Owls right here in the busy urbanscape — golf courses, ball fields, local airparks, community college greenswards, biking trails, freeway landscaping, and of course the non-green parts of the wash itself.

Since our move here in the late 1970s we had observed Burrowing Owl colonies in each and all of those seven microenvironments. Our present observation point was alongside one of the greens on a local golf course, and the owls' presence seemed almost enough to forgive the developers one of their cardinal sins here in the parched southwestern deserts — one-hundred golf courses, give or take a handful, were now available here in the greater Phoenix area to golfers and Burrowing Owls alike.

My immediate concern, regarding all four of the young ones of both species present, was errant golf balls. Of secondary concern was not creating disruption or distraction, which might lead players or course management to extricate the birds from their home. "Home" for this particular family was a washout underneath the cart path. Their burrow was as wide as the entire cart path and perhaps ten inches deep beneath the six-inch concrete, which provided the "roof" over their heads. Inconceivable as it was to me that many golfers had not observed the owls or realized they were at home in this burrow, it was even more inconceivable that the constant foot and cart traffic above and around the owls had not disconcerted them to the point of leaving. Perhaps the saving grace for the owls was the proximity of the green itself. A golfer leaving a green is typically either so pumped or so steamed that the presence of a ten-inch bird is of no consequence.

Burrowing Owl
Athene cunicularia

Most frequently heard vocalization
2 syllables, "*Hoo hooooooo*," high yet mellow (higher tone than mourning dove's *coo*)

Size
A medium-sized owl, 9.5" long with a 21" wingspan; approximately the size of a robin.

Most notable physical features
• often seen by day standing erect on ground or on posts
• round, flat head; yellow eyes
• long legs; stubby tail
• long, narrow wings
• bobs and bows when agitated

Seasonal movement
Permanent resident with some southward migration at northern limits of its range

Nest sites
Ground burrows of colonial rodents and other animals

Habits
Nocturnal but often encountered perched at burrow entrance or low post during morning and late afternoon daylight hours

Range/habitat
Burrowing Owls live in open, treeless areas in the Western U.S. and Florida; they are often found on golf courses and airports

EVIN MOVED. The spell was broken. Fledglings stumbled all over themselves in their scramble to return to the safety of their burrow. In the corner of my eye I caught movement from the next tee. An adult owl, probably beginning the evening's hunt along a natural area below the tee, had seen the movement around the nest and had flown to a horizontal branch in a mesquite, fifteen feet off the ground.

Keeping low, we duckwalked up the slope, then turned toward the mesquite at an angle meant to bring us closer to the parent without unduly alarming it. The next group of people with clubs was approaching the nest green anyway. It had been time to leave. Seeing the adult bird in the tree was a closer match for the bumbles' owl expectations, but I explained to them we were dispelling a myth — just as non-birders never expect to see owls on the ground, many birders never expect to see Burrowing Owls in a tree.

Along the greenbelt over the years we have observed Burrowing Owls roosting in trees, hunting from trees, and calling territorially from trees. We have also seen them doing all these things from fence wires, fence posts, ball field backstops, cement block walls, sani-cans, and elevated sprinkler heads — environmental opportunism from an owl tribe that has learned to be opportunistic in its brush with man and has never read the guide books.

The earliest known and longest continuously used "burrow" on the greenbelt is a plastic drainpipe beneath a busy sidewalk at the local community college. It diverts excess irrigation water from the lawn, underneath the concrete, to an asphalt parking lot. It appears to be about ten inches in diameter… perfect for a ten-inch bird. One spring when groundskeepers repainted the parking curbs from yellow to red,

The Burrowing Owl uses old burrows of squirrels, prairie dogs, other rodents, and even turtles. Only rarely are they excavated by the owl itself.

Burrowing Owl

both adults using this burrow bore red paint on their scapular feathers for several months until prebasic molt was completed at summer's end.

The bumbles, with their sharp eye for shapes and sizes, were surprised that these owls, which were obviously too tall for their burrow when standing upright, could disappear into that small an opening so easily. When shown that what appears to be the "knee" joint between a bird's tibia and tarsus actually corresponds to our ankle joint, they were more understanding. Apparently an ideal burrow for this owl is one too compact to allow upright posture, but no human adult with any mileage on their knees will understand this at all.

Burrowing Owls are known to take rodents and small birds, though we have never seen them do so on the greenbelt. We've

A typical brood is six to nine eggs, although there can be as many as twelve. The care of the young while still in the nest is performed by the male. At 14 days, the young may be seen roosting at the entrance to the burrow, waiting for the adults to return with food. They leave the nest at about 44 days and begin chasing living insects when 50-55 days old.

assumed they were subsisting here on large insects and the occasional lizard. Indeed, we have found pellets containing the apparent exoskeletons of beetles and grasshoppers. But this is a medium-sized owl, not a small one, and any close look through a spotting scope will reveal talons easily imagined carrying off prey up to the size of a young prairie dog.

We have seen Burrowing Owls throughout the west in natural settings (the prairies of Eastern Washington and the plains of Colorado), and in "semi-natural" settings (hay bales around the Salton Sea and agricultural canals throughout central Arizona). Until we experienced the bumbles' reactions to our greenbelt neighbors, we had always lamented the changes that rendered this species less "wild," forced them to live "with us," stripped them of their "owlness."

For JP and Devin, on vacation and coming as they were from days spent in sports camps, on playgrounds, and in front of computer games, the field trip to these owls, albeit city owls, was awesome. Everything these days is "awesome," but have you looked it up in a dictionary lately: *an emotion of mingled reverence, dread, and wonder; respect tinged with fear.*

Surely, if all the ancient myths are credible, this perfectly defines what our human ancestors felt in the presence of owls. Surely, if we are to retain our "humanness," we must instill in our young a sense of the natural world from which we have evolved. To know where they are going, to make good choices, it would seem essential they know from whence they came. And it is essential for them to know that the place from whence they came is so vastly different from where they now find themselves.

If JP and Devin retain an interest in the natural world into adulthood, they will seek out the wilderness owls — high mountains, higher latitudes. If not, and for now, they have been initiated. They have seen owls. They know "owl." "Owl" has form and breath. They have seen the talons. They have felt the wonder. City born and city bred, the four of them. Better here than not at all.

Opposite: The most common call is given only by adult males mainly when near the burrow to attract a female. A two-syllable "who-who" is given at the entrance of a promising burrow; this call is also associated with breeding and territory defense. Above: Burrowing Owl wing from above and below.

Chapter Twelve
Whiskered Screech-Owl

The Whiskered Screech-Owl is similar to the Western Screech-Owl, although it is slightly smaller and has noticeable "whiskers." In the field, however, they can only be reliably distinguished by their calls. The Whiskered Screech-Owl has slower, more evenly spaced notes in its call in contrast to the Western Screech-Owl's speeded up "bouncing ball." Additionally, the Whiskered Screech is primarily found in southern Arizona and Mexico, and typically at a higher elevation than Western Screech-Owls.

The Incident in Secret Canyon

BEEP-BEEP. BEEP-BEEP. Beep-beep. Beep-beep. Listen! An Owl? No, it's the freaking alarm clock! Midnight! No one moves. The beeping persists, reminiscent of some nightmare utility truck backing up to dump reality on an unfinished dream. Finally there is mumbling. Nothing intelligible. Nothing printable in a family chronicle of owling.

We have spent the morning bushwhacking a streamside without benefit of a fisherman's trail. We have spent the afternoon hiking up into the nearby wilderness area. We have crawled into our bags, wiped out by fatigue, at 8 p.m., and set the alarm for four hours hence. We are still unsophisticated enough to assume the strictly nocturnal owl species are most active in the middle of the night rather than just after dusk and just before dawn. We are still naive enough to assume a Whiskered Screech-Owl is going to come to our taped calls just because we are in the right place at the right time and badly want to find one on our own.

Arizona, arguably regarded as the premier birding destination in the country, rightly renowned for its hummingbirds, its Mexican breeders at the northern limits of their range, and its always-anticipated Mexican vagrants, is not considered an owling destination. This, despite the ease of finding Smitty's Scheelite Canyon Spotted Owls, probably the lifers for a majority of listers who have ticked this species. This, despite Elf Owl being much easier to find in Arizona's southeastern mountain ranges than in neighboring New Mexico and Texas. This, despite all the seemingly perfect desert habitat begging the Ferruginous Pygmy-Owl question until colonies in Kenedy County, Texas, recently became more widely known.

Here's a secret. Arizona is *the best* owling destination in the country. Thirteen of the nineteen North American owl species occur in Arizona, and a fourteenth is suspected and searched for because pockets of proper habitat exist. A few years back a team of best state birders found eleven species in one twenty-four hour period during springtime.

I AM A CONFIRMED morning person. I love to get up early, doing dawn with all my senses, but not on four hours of sleep, and midnight is not dawn. Deva is an avowed night owl. She loves to sleep in, luxuriating in the half-slumber of a slow awakening. She hates alarm clocks, and midnight is a bedtime for her, not a wake up call. Our

The ear tufts of the Whiskered Screech-Owl may or may not be visible in the field.

companion, BB, is a notorious sleepyhead, able to nap anytime, anyplace, on a moment's notice, always grumpy at abrupt arousals.

The three of us have come to see what we can find, after dark, in this Arizona mountain canyon, a secret canyon that shall remain unnamed. It is frequented mostly by herp and entomology researchers, and by hikers. It is not frequented by birders because it is relatively difficult to find, there are canyons much closer to civilized amenities that have all the much-sought specialties of the area, and access roads are periodically impassable due to weather conditions.

In later years, when we have become more fluent in the languages of owls and the nuances of this canyon, we regularly can count eight species of owls between canyon mouth and mountaintop, not on a single visit, but with luck and over the course of a summer. On this night, early in our relationship with the area, our modest goal is Whiskered Screech-Owl, reputedly common here.

We have neither heard nor seen anything, owl-wise, in our day-long rambles. Our faith is not strong. BB in particular is ambivalent in his enthusiasm, finding owls fascinating yet spooky. I am not at all certain we can roust him from his sleeping bag for the search, having heard him muttering to himself about roaming about in the dark and the possibility of bears — misgivings common to most novice owlers happy enough with the thought of owls and the idea of owling, but not at all comfortable with an actual search through dark and secret canyons.

What is it they say in the old Westerns: "We've got it to do." I sit up groggily, rubbing my eyes. Deva's bag is stirring. There is no movement yet from our friend's bag, but that is the source of the mumbling. Over his vehement protestations we have slept with the side door of the van wide open, wishfully thinking owl-song might awaken us, surely hoping we wouldn't awake to a snuffling bear or some other uninvited canyon critter.

Our initial and only sighting to date of a Whiskered Screech-Owl had come several years before on an Audubon

Whiskered Screech-Owl
Otus trichopsis

Most frequently heard vocalization
Steady series of soft, mellow "*Hoo*" notes, some long, some short, on an even pitch; often likened to Morse code

Size
A small owl, 7.25" long with a 18" wingspan; smaller than Western Screech-Owl, with small feet

Most notable physical features
• prominent ear tufts
• light underparts with heavy streaking and heavy barring
• pale bill
• yellow eyes

Seasonal movement
Non-migratory; permanent resident

Nest sites
Woodpecker holes and natural tree cavities

Habits
Nocturnal

Range/habitat
Whiskered Screech-Owls are found in dense pine-oak forests at higher elevations than Western Screech-Owls; their range in the U.S. is southern Arizona and southwestern New Mexico

Society field trip led by a ranger finely tuned to the fauna and flora of this isolated mountain range. Now we are again working through our owl list trying to find them all ourselves. Our tape recorder, with Whiskered's high, staccato toots, often likened to Morse code, has been set up, ready to go, as we prepared for bed. Whiskereds, like many of the small owls, typically are easy to "call up."

Reaching in the dark for the incessant alarm, I give the muttering sleeping bag a playful kick. As expected, growling emits from the depths of the bag, followed by a retaliatory kick. The alarm is off now and safely in my hand, but the aimless jab from our friend's bag knocks the recorder out the door into the moonlit clearing beside the van. The "play" switch lands just right, on stick or rock, and immediately *"Booo, booo, booo, booo-boo"* emanates from the unfazed machine.

Listen! What's that? It's a whiskered! Deva is half out of her bag now, yawning resignedly but listening intently. BB sheepishly explains to her what has happened as I grope for the tape, hit the "off" switch, and we all collapse wearily back on top of our bags. I repeat my movie line and peer outside at the stark illumination of a now fully-risen moon. "It looks like a great night for it."

Legend has long persisted that owlers best go owling on nights of a full moon. Many reasons have been espoused, most of them apocryphal — moonlight triggers hooting instincts, causing owls to more readily answer; owls see better by moonlight, enabling them to more easily find the caller; full moon activates male owls' hormones, arousing them to investigate the imagined rival; full moon scrambles the owlers' brain chemistry, dictating crazy behavior. Though this last certainly bears much scrutiny, it seems the real reason for this tradition is simply that the owler can more readily see the owl if it comes calling through moonlight rather than in total darkness.

We discuss these ideas as we fumble for our clothes. BB's theory is that owls, being ephemeral creatures of the night, are genetically programmed to scare people witless, and that since moonlight creates ciphers, shadows, and illusions not discerned in

Opposite: The Whiskered Screech-Owl is the smallest of the three screech-owls found in North America. Its facial "whiskers" give rise to its name. These bristles are more numerous and longer (extending well beyond the bill) than in the other screech-owls.

Whiskered Screech-Owl

total darkness, the owls just know that appearing in moonlight is more frightening to their human seekers. Deva is chuckling silently, for we know our companion, deep within his owl-awe, is totally serious. And he knows tonight's gibbous moon is a propitious sign.

Booo, booo, booo, booo-boo. Booo, booo, booo, booo, booo, booo-boo. Hello! With a flashback to that long-ago night in Iowa, I grab the recorder, jam it to my ear, then hold it up with thumbs down, and grin wildly. Three sleepy, bumbling agnostics are immediately transfixed, faithful converts, eyes wide, hands cupped behind their ears, crunch time as all three tumble together through a door designed for one. The owl is right there in an alligator juniper at the edge of the clearing, not twenty feet out,

The Whiskered Screech-Owl is believed to be entirely sedentary. Most of the population is far enough south that it is unaffected by winter weather. In the north of its range (Arizona) there may be some downslope movements in winter.

Whiskered Screech-Owl

bathed in moonlight, erasing the need for either binoculars or searchbeam. Its closeness and clarity bring us up short, arms and legs immobilized, mid-stride, in angles and postures not usually associated with fully ambulatory human beings.

Booo, booo, booo, booo-boo. Booo, booo, booo, booo, booo, booo-boo.

Frozen, fearing sudden movement will break the spell, we scrutinize a Whiskered Screech-Owl scrutinizing back at us. Small, ear tufts, yellow eyes… wait, it's not calling. But something is! We glance around. Another identical apparition awaits on a slightly higher branch, ten feet to the left of the first. It is not calling either. But something is! Movement skirts the periphery of moonlight, disappearing behind the van. A Whiskered is back there for sure, tooting out their Morse code. An answer comes from our right. Another shadow slips out

This owl's diet consists mainly of moths, beetles, spiders, and grasshoppers, with centipedes being an important winter food. Whiskereds usually hunt from a perch in a tree where it will fly out to catch winged prey. It will also fly back and forth in treetops catching multiple insects.

of the oaks, materializing next to our original bird.

There is Morse code all around us. Whiskereds call in duet, moving, resettling, sliding in and out of moonlight, transmogrifying into pine knots and oak snags, then back again into owls! Now we are moving, conversing, first in whispers, then conversationally, talking ourselves down, trying to account, guesstimate, decipher what we are seeing. The tape recorder is long forgotten, silent, buried somewhere in the scrum of sleeping bags, only that one brief snip of code, as tape impacted ground, having conjured this convention of spirits, shifting and shuffling through the shadows.

A ROUND THE NEXT morning's campfire the three of us fervently reaffirm that we did not simultaneously enjoy three identical owldreams. Here is what we know for sure. Whiskereds are margin-

The nocturnal Whiskered Screech-Owl is about the size of a bluebird. The color of the Arizona birds is generally light gray, but becomes increasingly reddish brown into its southern range in Mexico.

ally smaller than Western Screech-Owls, with noticeably smaller feet because rodents and birds comprise a miniscule portion of their diet compared to Westerns. They live higher in the mountains than westerns, generally above 5,000 feet. They like mixed stands of oak and pine like their cousin, the Flammulated Owl.

Here is what we think we know. We had at least five visitors. Perhaps we have camped at the intersection of two territories, each with its own pair, perhaps with an odd unmated bird just passing by, still hopeful, still searching. Each of us had counted at least three owls at once while hearing an unseen bird calling. At least one of us claims five birds visually, if shadows can be counted, if shadows of owls can be discernably distilled from shadows of whatever else is out there in the night.

Whatever else is out there in the night is where BB's appreciation and fascination with owls bumps up against his apprehension and foreboding, an almost child-like instinct that couples his desire to find and know with his dread of the finding and the knowing. Simply put, he finds owl venues scary territory, and he makes no apologies to us for his feelings. Still, when he finds that I will include a chapter on the incident in secret canyon in my owl project, he asks that I not divulge his real name. He has certain circles of friends who might not understand that a person of his reputed backcountry acumen and skill feels a little shaky thrashing around in the dead of night chasing ghosts.

I propose a trade-off. I will not use his full name if he promises never to divulge the exact name or location of the canyon. Deva and I have returned many times since that Whiskered episode, both with and without BB. On one magical night we had four species of owls right in our favorite campsite. Welcome to Oregon — now go home. We would like to keep this canyon to ourselves.

I HAVE SUGGESTED TO BB that his sense of fear and dread about the owls on our periphery does not make him less human, but moreso. From time immemorial man has drunk this cloudy emotional brew in the presence of the nightstalkers. I have encouraged him to return sometime by himself and spend the night alone, cleansing himself of his fears, much like ancient tribesmen on a vision quest. He could commune with the Whiskereds, come to a celebration of their natural beauty and adaptive traits, become comfortable with the more nebulous and mysterious aspects of their darker side. We have even offered to drop him off, leave him, pick him up the next morning. He will have none of it. It seems that for him, owls' nebulous and mysterious darker side is stronger medicine than their natural beauty and adaptive traits.

The Whiskered Screech and the Western Screech-Owl do not seem to intermingle in habitat, and there seems to be a clear division between the two owls as you rise in elevation. The Whiskered Screech inhabits up into the pine zone of the Montane habitat, where it comes in contact with the Flammulated Owl, and down into the upper Sonoran zone where there is a significant overlap with the Elf Owl.

Chapter Thirteen

Long-Eared Owl

A Note About Poetry and Owls: This chapter of Long-eared Owl obser-vations is written as poetry. If your experiences with poetry in school were like mine, your instructors spent a lot of time asking you to interpret exactly what the poets were trying to say... and killing for you the "wild and free" that poetry should be. Exactly what the poet means is nothing compared to what-ever the poem might mean to you. Like our raptors, poetry is the stuff of imag-ination. It should soar. It should explore the edges of the light and conjure questions of the night. What better medium for owls than poetry? What bet-ter vehicle for poetry than owls?

The Long-Eared Chronicles

Fire, Talon, Tooth

Moxee City, Washington
March 19, 1978

We came down from the passes way early this year
As soon as the last three branchers had learned to fly.
Now the light is returning, telling its season,
But my gift says our time on old Blewett is done —
We have watched as the lightning and fire filled the sky.

The nest belonged to old raven, perfect it seemed,
With meadow voles plenty in Naneum nearby,
But the forest was old growth, the Icon lived there,
Bringing the longeyes, and greenmen in their green trucks —
Too much noise and disturbance for a tribe so shy.

Long-eared Owl

Six eggs I set down, and my male preened me so well,
Finally a mate who would stay and make roost close by.
But one day he flushed at the sound of men's metal,
Slipping through the pine boughs, seeking quieter perch —
And the movement caught a Cooper's sharp roving eye.

Alone now, by myself at incubation's height
With all my hunting and feeding to satisfy,
Leaving the nest untended with bandits about,
I returned in the dark to find the Quilled One there —
I chased it away, too late, with my shrill cat cry.

Four left to fledge, four to initiate and teach,
And the forest turning green to brown, tinder dry,
Till late lightseason storms lit the prairies below,
And one of them disappeared on that fiery night —
Smoke and haze blown all the way up to mountain high.

The fire brought the axe men, hacking their random lines,
And the huge, whirling noiseflies, spewing foam, flew nigh.
My gift cried escape and we flew down, skirting flames,
Coming home again to dark-season shrubsteppe pines —
With elders and cousins, aunts and kin to ally.

A longeyes was here today, and brought his young one.
Quiet, respectful, their species they did belie.
Bearing apples for the horses, their writing sticks
Noting perch and posture, counting us one by one —
Then, in hushed tones, they interred the fallen magpie.

Opposite: The Long-eared Owl is a medium-sized owl with conspicuous ear tufts. They appear slim and slouch forward when perched. When roosting, a Long-eared Owl will stretch its body to make itself appear like a tree branch.

Long-Eared Owl
Asio otus

Most frequently heard vocalization
A long, extended, moaning "*Hoooooo*" note; also a cat-like whine

Size
A medium-sized owl, 15" long with a 36" wingspan; approximately the size of a crow

Most notable physical features
• long, prominent ear tufts
• elongated, slender posture
• underparts streaked lengthwise
• buffy orange facial disk with dark vertical stripe through eye
• yellow eyes
• often roosts in groups

Seasonal movement
Some migration to colonial roosting sites in winter and as prey species fluctuate; those migrating are thought to be younger birds

Nest sites
Stick platforms and abandoned crow and squirrel nests in trees

Habits
Nocturnal

Range/habitat
Long-eared Owls are found in forests and woodlands throughout the U.S. and Canada, with the exception of the southeastern states

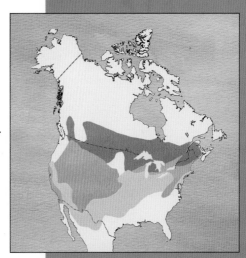

Long-eared Owls are buoyant fliers, appearing to glide noiselessly even when their wings are flapping. They are very maneuverable and can fly through fairly dense brush. They fly moth-like, often hovering and fluttering while looking for prey.

Urban Retreat

North Mountain Park, Arizona
December 31, 1992

Snows blew to the Tonto early this moon,
Pushing us down to low deserts unknown.
Led by an old female, arrived alone,
Who swore she was versed in our ancient rune.
Off at sundrop, evading raptors' wrath,
On long, flat wings, deep wingbeats, light loading,
Long glides toward bright lights brought some foreboding,
To mesquite bosque beside well-worn path.
Not dense, the grove's thermal cover suspect,
But desert's warmth seemed not to dissipate
And hosts of mice her choice did validate
As we fed and found roostlimbs to inspect.
Suncome found us, eight in number, sleeping—
Safe roost, dream visions of shortlight keeping.

In blackness, gifted with keenest vision,
By light we seek the utmost solitudes.
Any din and stir any roost precludes.
And here we awoke to great commotion.
An odd species that hooted, walked and ran,
Led on lines by the hairy barking one
Wending through desert mazes overrun,
Yet gave no heed to us or to our plan.
And then this night's hunt so interrupted
By shooting lights and concussive sound
That rent the sky and shook the ground,
We flinched in fear and to the bosque fled.
But the old female remained calm of mien —
And reminded us we were still unseen.

Long-eared Owl

Until a barker vented at a perch
And its walker glanced up and saw, despite
The streaks and bars and upright posture sleight,
Golden orbs, eartufts, and the whitewash smirch.
Word was out, for longeyes have their network.
Some amongst us have sung its force before.
At first a few, then groups with many more,
First some distance, even by dark they lurk.
Then some come close, harassing us to flush,
Perhaps to hear our call and see our flight,
Until there is no peace by dark or light
And searchers prowl beneath in underbrush.
Our gift now says forego these ridicules —
Gladly we fly this colony of fools.

A Long-eared Owl's ear tufts may be completely invisible when they are laid down, as they are in flight. The owl's colors are similar to the Great Horned Owl, although its slender shape, smaller size, large, round, orangish facial disk, and cross-barred chest set it apart.

Long-eared Owls inhabit open woodlands, forest edges, riparian strips along rivers, hedgerows, juniper thickets, woodlots, and wooded ravines and gullies. Breeding habitat must include thickly-wooded areas for nesting and roosting with nearby open spaces for hunting. Overall populations are thought to be declining in North America because of the loss of riparian nesting habitat through urban and agricultural development. Useful habitat enhancements include retention of fallow fields, elimination of vast monocultures, decreased use of pesticides, and planting of conifer groves.

Some Say Sorcerer

Owl Pond, Dinetah
September 24, 1994

The old one came to me today — almost a year.
Some say him shaman, some say him priest or singer.
Both of us elders, both of us our tribes revere.
I teach to him our songs. He sings me sorcerer.

Around his weathered waist, he hangs the sacred pouch
With withered claw of bat and skull of mountain vole.
Amulets he has gleaned through years beneath my perch
To cleanse dine skinwalkers and speed the soiled soul.

Today I bark him *oo-ack*, the high-pitched alarm
For the Great Horned Ones roaming night in the Chuskas.
Today I squeal him *ya-ow*, sensing future harm
From his people who no longer need to know us.

There is no water here, three long-light seasons now,
But still we gather in these tangled tamarisks,
For more eyes more efficient hunting does endow
In our short-light season with its communal risks.

Down from Black Mesa winds, down canyons of San Juan,
To prey abundance found feeding fields of the tribe
Who, like our species, on all sides are set upon
By a culture whose values they cannot subscribe.

The old one a dream describes, come in this moondance.
He saw the longeyes come to me, numbering five,
Seeking ancient rhythms, chasing a final chance
To learn past pathways, and keep our old ways alive.

Long-eared Owl

Just yesterday they came, proving his gift still strong.
Three male ones, the two here often in years before:
Short one, Peabody truck, he searches all day long.
Tall one, words papers, no one knows my species more.

Two females, one long hair, old one say Cherokee,
Small one, great round white wizard's eye he has shouldered.
Old one's dream say stay my perch, let him picture me.
His sign sings me from the shadows, helps spread the word.

*Long-eared Owl wing from
above and below.*

I Am Raptor

Yaqui Well, California
February 6, 1999

Shriek it down the mountainface, sing it down the wind.

I have soared with ravens, my gift they can't exscind.

Odd, the elders say, for last year's brancher to be the sacred scribe,

When priests and poets convene and winter-call the tribe.

Too young, they say, and much too restless for our kind,

But certainly the genes bode well, even through instincts unrefined.

My grandfather, in the Coachella, twenty-five long years from fledging,

When he was struck by a Rough-legged, so the songs alleging,

And my mother, so dark and buff they called her Cara Roja, largest in the band,

Until she slashed the egg bandit whose claws and fangs she did withstand.

Now she is known as Coonkills, and young females vie for her old nests,

Long-eared Owl

And she has schooled me well, as my wisdom of our rituals attests.
Call it down Coyote Creek, hail it down hunting place,
I have flown the thermals, my gift they can't efface.

Odd, the elders say, that I was nurtured in the egg a full five weeks,
Days more than usual, in the cliff-niche nest above the creeks.
There I learned to squeal the soft *ee-uh* on nights unstarred
To speed my father with pocket gopher and lizards barred.
And I mimicked my mother's soft, nasal *shoo-oogh* at his prolonged absence,
Snapped my bill and distended feathers when danger called for this pretense.
Now I scribe her new mate's courtship, with wing-clapping and zig-zag flight replete.
I hear the deep *hoo-hoo*, slow and well-spaced, which the breeding males repeat.
I've watched her lead him down the valley to the site she seeks,
And I've seen them head-to-head, working gently with their beaks.

Scream it down the hot springs, hoot it down bubbling wells,
I have taken prey, my gift all the myth dispels.

Odd, the elders say, that I was sent to ones so retiring and so shy,
Of whom the longeyes know so little they know not the where or why.
And even songbirds our roosts and haunts do not disclose
Since we rarely prey on them or bother their repose.
But troubles stalk us, even so, as our riparian groves are lost,
And I was sent to proselytize, eschewing not the cost.
When longeyes come, the elders counsel caution and retreat
While I alone perch sentinel to learn and teach and meet.
One came today, moving slowly under giant wizard's eye he could scarcely lift.
I sat in dappled sunlight as he clicked his superficial images with which to sing my gift.

Cry it down the canyons, sough it down the willow,
I am raptor, my gift they don't yet feel or know.

Opposite: Long-eared Owls hunt mainly from late dusk to just before dawn, flying low to the ground, with the head canted to one side listening for prey. When prey is spotted, the owl pounces immediately, pinning the prey to the ground with its powerful talons.

Chapter Fourteen
Northern Pygmy-Owl

The Northern Pygmy-Owl, like all pygmy-owls, is diurnal (active in the daytime). It is a small but very bold and ferocious predator that will attack prey more than twice its size. Unlikely to be confused with any other owl, it is often seen as the lead bird in a cloud of screaming (mobbing) song birds. It also has a distinctive, low, evenly-spaced tooting call that makes finding it among other daytime birds easier.

The Sun Gnome

AS WASHINGTON STATE ROUTE 20 drops out of the North Cascades, it escapes the tight canyons of the Skagit River and begins to transect pasture land bordered by woodlots of big trees. In our rear-view mirror was the largest winter convention of bald eagles in the lower forty-eight, congregating as they did every year to feast on spawned out salmon along the upper Skagit. Up ahead a shrike left its fencepost lookout, coursed a low, rapid line along the weedy road shoulder and then dropped abruptly from sight. Strike!

As we neared the spot, trying to count fenceposts, I slowed the van and three noses pressed against the rain streaked passenger windows, three pairs of eyes hoping to pierce the misty gloaming for a glimpse of the action. It was a typical late afternoon in a typical Pacific Northwest February. Sundown with no sun.

Spooked by the vehicle as we drew abreast, the bird lifted, laboriously it seemed, into a small bare tree and paused in perfect

silhouette against the background of gray sky as we flashed by. From tiny daggered talons hung a mouse, tail down, already dispatched. It took a moment for the perfection of the silhouette to maneuver the synapses from blurry vision to full understanding. *Stop! Turn Around! That was NOT a shrike!*

A moment at fifty miles per hour on a mist-slicked highway is approximately fifty yards. Checking traffic, slowing, braking, taking out small plants on both shoulders while making an illegal u-turn — that's another fifty or so. One hundred yards was about the time I needed to decide if little people aged 11 and 6 would be turned on or turned off by a close encounter with an owl doing exactly what an owl was born and bred to do. Northern Pygmy-Owl. Our first Northern Pygmy-Owl. It was an easy decision.

The tree was now on the driver's side. I crawled the van, in gear but with no acceleration, back toward the bird as Deva scrambled for the camera. She handed it to me with a small telephoto lens attached. As I rested the lens on the side mirror and focused, she steered from the passenger side. This maneuver is not recommended in any of the driving manuals, but we were well practiced at it nonetheless.

Twenty yards, little or no ambient light left in the "sunset;" fifteen yards, not a blip from the light meter; ten yards, the owl glares and shifts its feet. "Now!" Deva cuts the ignition as I depress the brake pedal. Click. Click. Two frames; goodbye owl. Raptors never suffer fools watching them eat. Not from this close. Warm mouse to go. As I pulled the lens off the side mirror, I saw two little faces, bug-eyed,

The Northern Pygmy-Owl's small size, plump shape, long narrow tail, bold white eyebrows, brown streaks on white under parts, and white spotting on a brown head and forehead make it very distinctive.

hanging out the window behind me, speechless. Grinning, I reflected upon what we had come to call a successful outdoor adventure — "a good day at the office."

The slides came back at the end of the week. Just as anticipated there were two frames of grossly underexposed owl, perfectly silhouetted, predator with prey, black on gray, a faintly purple cast to the whole affair. Other than the lack of ear tufts and the longish tail (the owl's, not the mouse's) the shots were in no way diagnostic of Northern Pygmy-Owl. No plumage characteristics, no eye color. Certainly not a "feather study," certainly not a habitat photo, but what we would euphemistically label an "art shot." None of the slick magazines dealing in crisp detail and vibrant color would have any interest, but a cool shot nevertheless. A perfect distillation of the essence of "owl" into stark, monochromatic simplicity. Not a portrait of Northern Pygmy-Owl but a portrait of "everyowl": preying; surviving; being.

In the darkroom I printed an 8x10 of everyowl, then printed another one overexposed enough to show some light mottling on the bird's chest and belly. I stuck both prints in the owl family album, catalogued the slides in the hanging file, and forgot about them for fifteen years.

THROUGHOUT OUR SEATTLE years after the silhouette with mouse, we saw Northern Pygmy-Owls more or less regularly. So regularly we never went out specifically to look for one, nor did it even occur to us to try to call one up. We saw them near the coast and on mountaintops. We saw them in suburban settings and in wilderness areas. At the remote and enchanting little Sunday Lake, snowshoeing in two feet of fresh powder, we watched one sit on its ten-foot-high perch as a screaming snowmobile passed directly beneath it. Pygmy-owls, a diurnal species, were a part of the Pacific Northwest landscape, a landscape shaped by a climate that often produced days so dark and dreary that even the more nocturnal of the owls were about before nightfall. Then we moved to Arizona.

Northern Pygmy-Owl
Glaucidium gnoma

Most frequently heard vocalization
Monotonous 1 or 2 syllable "*Hoo*" or "*Hoo-hoo*" notes repeated at regular one- to two-second intervals

Size
A small owl, 7" long with a 12" wingspan; approximately the size of a sparrow

Most notable physical features
• compact and small
• no ear tufts
• long tail with narrow, white bars
• yellow eyes
• pygmy-owls can often be located by watching for scolding songbirds

Seasonal movement
Sedentary with some altitudinal migration in winter

Nest sites
Woodpecker holes and natural tree cavities

Habits
Diurnal

Range/habitat
Northern Pygmy-Owls are found in conifer and mixed forests from 5,000 to 10,000 feet in the western mountains of the U.S. and Canada

On this little owl's nape are two distinctive, vertical black patches that resemble an extra pair of eyes.

LIFELONG BIRDERS ALL understand that once an elusive species has been painstakingly found, it then becomes easy to find or, indeed, it begins to find the birder even without being sought. Much less generally understood is that if an elusive species is initially chanced upon unsought, subsequent sightings can take years of searching and frustration.

With its long, bright days, harsh, barren landscapes, and three specialty species of small owls, Arizona dictated a different kind of owling — less casual, more focused — and it definitely is a nighttime endeavor. But we knew Northern Pygmy-Owls inhabited the higher altitudes throughout the state. All the field guides and all our new birding friends alluded to it. And sure enough, right away we began hearing pygmy-owls on most of our outings. Our very first encounter, in upper Madera Canyon of the Santa Ritas, typified our first several years of searching for Northern Pygmy-Owls in Arizona.

It was springtime and we were hiking a well-used trail up-canyon, hoping for migrant warblers, when we heard a familiar tooting — staccato and monotonous, too low and harsh for Townsend's Solitaire, and too slow and nasal for rock squirrel. It could only be a pygmy-owl and it seemed just around the next bend. We stopped and whispered out a plan. The next stretch of canyon was steep and still in shadow, but the bird sounded relatively low. Stealthily we crept around a house-sized boulder, all four binoculars at the ready to glass up the slopes, thrilled that we were so quickly to renew an old acquaintanceship in these new surroundings.

He was right there in front of us! An elderly gentleman leaning against a tree, binoculars in hand, mimicking a Northern Pygmy-Owl so well we couldn't believe he wasn't playing a tape or concealing an owl in his pocket. He too was after migrant spring passerines, hoping to entice them to "mob" the pygmy-owl they thought they were hearing. It's hard to say which of us was more embarrassed, but before we could stammer through introductions and explanations, the mob indeed found the "pygmy owl" — many chickadees and titmice, a flycatcher, two creepers, a redstart, an Olive Warbler, and the prize of the day, a Black-and-white Warbler, which proved to be the prize of the entire spring.

It became a too often repeated scenario — other birders imitating Northern Pygmies to lure in other birds or us imitating Northern Pygmies to lure in an owl but getting … other birds. From the late 1970s through the entire decade of the 1980s, long after we had enjoyed Elf, Whiskered Screech, and even Ferruginous Pygmy, the Arizona specialty owls, long after we had seen twelve of the state's thirteen possible owl species,

At rest, a Northern Pygmy-Owl sits with its tail cocked away from vertical, and often twitches its tail when excited. In flight, they resemble shrikes with rapid wing beats and rounded wing tips.

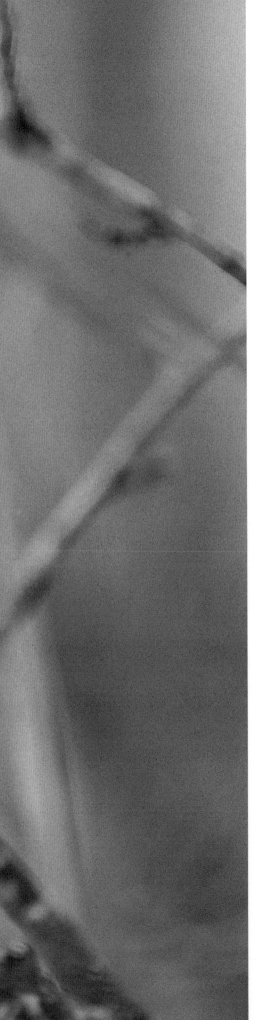

and long after we had emptied our own nest of young owlers, we had still not seen a Northern Pygmy-Owl in Arizona.

We did not realize it at first, but as Monson and Phillips in their seminal work, *The Birds Of Arizona*, pointed out, "*Glaucidium gnoma* is generally uncommon… the foraging area of each pair is very large in Arizona, where the birds are far less abundant than Screech-Owls and Elf Owls, or even Horned Owls." The seven-inch Pygmy would be smaller than the six-inch Elf were it not for the two inches of its relatively long tail. The species name, *gnoma*, comes to us from the Greek verb *gnome* —to know — and is associated in Greek legends with Athena, the goddess of wisdom.

Elliott Coues, who first described Northern Pygmy-Owl, was one of America's earliest and best ornithologists. Well grounded in classical studies, he knew, as we have today forgotten, that gnomes in ancient lore were not simply creatures of diminutive stature but the guardians of knowledge and superstitionary rituals. He may well have chosen his new owl's scientific name upon hearing a tale of Nootka oral tradition during his travels around Puget Sound in the late nineteenth century:

Raven was originally a white bird. He was cunning and courageous but was continually preyed upon by the thunderbird who lived at the top of the mountain. Raven took on black feathers and hid the sun behind clouds and fog so the thunderbird couldn't find him. Owls, quiet and secretive by nature, observe many things and are very wise. Owl-Who-Hunts-By-Day had watched Raven and knew where Raven had hidden the sun. He also knew when the thunderbird slept. Every few weeks a tribesman would go to a special tree and mimic the owl's soft hooting. Owl-Who-Hunts-By-Day would appear, and if the thunderbird was asleep the owl would blow the clouds and fog from in front of the sun so the Nootkas could enjoy sunshine until thunderbird awoke.

CLOUDS AND FOG were not the problem in Arizona, but finding an uncommon seven-inch bird in its square-mile territory proved daunting, especially in mountainous terrain

About 90 percent of this owl's diet is comprised of small mammals and birds. It will kill birds such as Gambel's or California Quail, or American Robins, that are more than twice its weight.

where those of us without wings are confined to canyon bottoms and creekbeds. Many times we followed reported sightings within twenty-four hours but were not rewarded. Many times we knew we were in the right places at the wrong times by the swiftness and vehemence of the local songbirds' response to our imitated calls. Birds comprise one-third of the Northern Pygmy-Owl's diet, a portion considerably larger than that of other small owls.

In June of 1991, hiking the South Fork of Cave Creek in the Chiricahua Mountains on the trail of the elusive Eared Trogon, predictably without the slightest owl-thought, we finally came unexpectedly upon our first Arizona Northern Pygmy-Owl. It was perched much higher than we had ever seen one, near the top of a towering ponderosa pine. So high it was but a silhouette. And this silhouette, like that on a long ago sundown also featured another life form. Swiveling its head from side to side to confront its tormentor, this pygmy-owl was being harassed by a Blue-throated Hummingbird, rhythmically zigging and zagging inches in front of the owl's face.

The Trogon eluded us, but I was now the proud owner of two artistically-interesting but technically-flawed Northern Pygmy-Owl photographs. Motivated primarily by environmental concerns, I had recently decided to dismantle my photography darkroom and go digital. Far cleaner and faster, supposedly allowing far more creative latitude, Adobe Photoshop had been our program of choice, but I was still a fumbling novice, still skeptical, still emotionally corded to the old witches' brew of sloppy, smelly poisons I had been concocting for a decade. I was still seeking some sign, some epiphany.

The owl/hummingbird image was much too distant and grainy to warrant blowing up, even on the computer. As I pulled the Northern Pygmy-Owl page from the slide drawer to file it away, I glanced again at the old owl/mouse silhouette beside it, delighting again in its crude perfection. Something about it, though, still gnawed at the outer reaches of my mind. Here was a graphic depiction of owl-life that obscured any real details of that life. That was truly the essence of owl — how little we really see, how little we need to see to know and imagine. And it was easy to imagine owls as first and favorite consorts of the earliest and wisest sorcerers.

THE WEEKEND BLEW UP a late summer monsoon, replete with gusting winds and lightning show. Edgy, despairing of birding in this weather, I flipped on the computer and idly watched it boot up as my consciousness once again booted up owl with mouse and conjured how it must have retreated to a secret place, then shredded and eaten its catch. Knowing there always seemed something missing in the spare image, yielding suddenly to the thrall of the owl/sorcerer in my head, I retrieved the old slide and ran it through the scanner. In a few seconds the owl was there again, on my monitor in Photoshop, mouse still dangling in cold purplish gray perfection after all these years.

Northern Pygmy-Owls are very secretive and tend to perch and roost in thickets where it is safe from predators. At times, one will sit atop the highest spire of a tree.

Postmodern, sterile version of mouse in hand, I began playing wizard with the software. A click on the "layers" option and a slide toward "brightness" — the owl and mouse receded into brighter but still dense fog. A slide toward "contrast" — the owl and mouse sharpened but were then obscured by enveloping darkness. The exact nature of an owl! And in my hand, scurrying here and there across the mouse-pad, the aptly-named plastic-over-wire mouse started bridging the gap between nature and technology, nature and postmodern man.

Mouse at work, "brightness" and "contrast" together — the owl and mouse came forward out of the persistent dusk in better relief, but still fuzzy. Still too much grain. Still no detail. Still the persistent knowledge that a computer cannot create color where none was seen, cannot conjure light from darkness, cannot fully illuminate to night-blind, flightless humans why and how owls do what they do.

The mouse scampered over to the "curves" option — a "powerful" tool, the tutorial stated. We would see. A click on curves' "blue" option and the mouse flitted down and to the right — purplish cast disappeared, shadows uniformly dispersed. Mouse darted to the top, then hurried left — the fog began to dissipate, leaving… blue. The mouse moved on — more may be better! The blue began to lighten, the old chemicals now truly obsolete, old darkroom images already surpassed.

Northern Pygmy-Owl wing from above and below.

The mouse leaped again. "Curves" *was* powerful! Mottling appeared on the owl's breast. Adrenaline began to stalk my whole body just as fifteen winters ago when I saw the owl from ten feet through the telephoto lens. The blue was now that of cloudless sky. The sorcerer was at work, without his stinking brew. Owl was the medium. The fogshroud seemed about to lift.

The mouse made one final jump. My old workshirt was damp under the arms. The sky was reducing to white with individual pixels of blue. Behind the owl's head, around the owl's head, there appeared a soft warm glow, a suffusion of lightness turning… yellow! It was circular!

The mouse twitched. As individual pixels of blue disappeared from the sky, pixels of yellow appeared and deepened within the circular suffusion. The owl was still a silhouette, but its head was now haloed, backlit by… the sun!

I unclutched the mouse and stared, transfixed, at the monitor. The adrenaline was now working between my shoulder blades and up along my scalp. The fog had been blown away. I had seen the light, had entered the computer age. Owl had spoken to me, had altered my landscapes. I had felt owl's breath, had seen owl's magic. I knew somewhere there was an ancient Nootka tribesman who understood.

The result of my adjustments to the Northern Pygmy-Owl with mouse image.

Chapter Fifteen
Northern Hawk Owl

The Northern Hawk Owl is not likely to be confused with any other owl. It is a strictly diurnal owl that is distinctly hawk-like or falcon-like in appearance. It is usually seen perched on a high vantage point scanning for prey. Very bold and almost tame, it sometimes may be approached very close with little obvious fear or concern of people.

Hawk Owl News

SUDDENLY THE OWL was there! Here, actually! Here, close, where an eye-blink before there had been no owl. Northern Hawk Owl! Always anticipated, but never fully expected. It is part of the birder's psyche to know that the harder-to-find target owl species, the denizens of the true wilderness of the far north or the far remote, just appear, as if conjured by sheer force of imagination.

We were in an old burn area in the taiga south of Churchill. There had been rumors. Hawk owl news travels like the birds themselves — hard to come by and hard to substantiate when heard. Ephemeral. Opaque. A desiccated pellet under a long-cold roost. A shadow through the sun-dappled tamaracks and spruce. Rumors of a nesting pair. Fledglings seen being fed. My pulse had quickened the previous day when an unknown fisherman along the river had answered my discreet inquiry with one of his own — "You're not a photographer are you?" *Shazam!* We were finally in the right place at the right time!

Northern Hawk Owl

We had blackened our hiking boots on three different vacations, tromping through forest burns for Northern Hawk Owl: southern British Columbia; northwestern Montana; and along Alaska's Glenn Highway. The reasons why breeding season reports of this seemingly-elusive owl are slow to reach the general birding public are as logical as why the reports often cite burn areas. Telephones and computers are hard to find in remote forests, but red-backed voles, the preferred prey species of the hawk owl, and other rodent prey are easy for the owls to find if fire has removed the forest understory. Once an owl family has depleted the prey population, it moves to another area, leaving behind only the rumors.

Our nearest miss had come one August in Glacier National Park. Smoke jumpers told us they had seen long-tailed owls within the week, hunting by day the margins of a small blaze they were working. Unfortunately, parts of the area were still smoldering and isolated hot spots dictated public closure. (As if other rumors of grizzlies in the area wouldn't have precluded any deep penetration into the backcountry anyway.)

IT IS ALWAYS FASCINATING yet hardly surprising how often bears and owls are intertwined in natural history lore, wilderness neighbors for the most part. Now here we were an hour north of a well-documented polar bear denning area along the western shore of Hudson Bay, raptly attentive to our life hawk owl, yet casting furtive glances over our shoulders from time to time.

Species name *ulula* in Latin, the owl before us now began to call in its odd, quavering vocalization, eerie, onomatopoeic, sounding like nothing so much as one of the falcons which it strongly resembles because of its long-tailed profile. A contact call to an unseen mate? A clarion call of a true wilderness indicator species instinctively celebrating its wildness? An alarm call announcing the two upright pilgrims encroaching into its domain?

Movement along the ground beneath a tangle of charred, fire-felled logs materialized amazingly into a dingy

Northern Hawk Owl
Surnia ulula

Most frequently heard vocalization
Series of whistles up to six seconds long, resembling "Ulululululu"; alarm a shrill "kikikiki" (like falcon)

Size
A medium-sized, hawk-like owl, 16" long with a 28" wingspan; smaller than a crow

Most notable physical features
- long, slender, pointed tail that gives bird a falcon-like appearance
- fine, horizontal barring on underparts
- broad black sideburns frame pale face; no ear tufts
- flies low and fast, with quick, stiff wingbeats
- swoops up to perch; often hovers

Seasonal movement
Permanent resident with irruptive movements depending on prey availability; rarely moves south in winter into northern U.S.

Nest sites
Most often in enlarged Northern Flicker or Pileated Woodpecker holes, tops or hollows of tree stumps, and occasionally in old nests of raptors or crows

Habits
Diurnal

Range/habitat
Boreal forests of Northern Hemisphere; conifer forests, birch scrub, tamarack bogs, muskeg

gray fuzzball, nearly the size of its parent, but tailless, scrabbling along through the cinders, soiling its fledgling down with soot. Even wilderness owl babies are babies, and anthropomorphism dies hard. Mom was going to be ticked!

Careful glassing through the debacle of black stumps and dead snags produced two more young owls. One, trying mightily to fly, fluttered halfway up a burned sapling leaning atop a pile of spruce rubble, then crash landed, upright, three feet off the ground, huge yellow pupils so wide in the dimly-lit and blackened forest it seemed only a caricature of a real owl. The other, apparently exhausted by its own similar efforts, was lying limp on its belly, draped like a wet rag over a nearby horizontal branch, head hanging off one side, miniature talons off the other. We

Opposite: This Northern Hawk Owl image compelled me to share the extraordinary world of owls with others. Above: The Hawk Owl's diet varies depending on the time of year. In summer, the majority of their diet consists of small rodents, especially voles. In winter, birds consist of as much as 90 percent of their food intake, with birds as large as Sharp-tailed, Willow, and Ruffed Grouse taken.

Young Hawk Owls leave the nest by the time they are three weeks old, but remain near the nest for about two months. They are not fully independent until they are about three months of age.

were sure it was dead, come to some premature demise, but when the ululations began anew, its head jerked up, baby yellows huge like its sibling's in their life and alertness.

Abruptly the calling stopped, and we swung our binoculars to the parent's perch just in time to see the adult bird drop onto the forest floor thirty yards beyond and disappear into a clump of new greenery. Not wishing to negatively impact this domestic scene in any way, and assuming the show was over, we began slowly backing out of the clearing. But the show was just beginning.

Almost before we could begin our retreat, the parent was winging back toward us. Low over the cleared burn, then with a final upward swoop, it resumed its original perch, so close we didn't need binoculars to grasp what we were seeing. Our jaws dropped and breathing stopped. Dangling from the owl's beak was the foot of a rabbit, a large foot with a bloodied mass of fur above the first joint where it had obviously just been detached from a warm body. Not the white foot of a snowshoe, but nearly that large and a light buffy tan, probably that of an Arctic hare.

Certainly aware of our presence but seemingly oblivious to it, the owl fixed us with a stare that, in this context, could only be described as baleful. (Anthropomorphism dies hard.) Transferring the rabbit's foot from beak to branch and securing it with one taloned foot, the owl proceeded to go about the business for which beak and claw were perfectly designed.

The Northern Hawk Owl inhabits open forests usually with easy access to clearings. It may be found at the edge of a burn or open areas cleared by lumbering. When in mountainous areas, it may move up as far as 6,000 feet in elevation.

We watched for a breathtaking moment, then guessing the young had been fed first, we tore ourselves from this once-in-a-lifetime scene, returning to the trail in stunned silence. We would never again question the placing of owls with the hawks under the designation of "raptor." We now knew "raptor" first-hand, had seen and experienced "raptor." From rumor to raptor in an eyeblink, Northern Hawk Owl was the link between these two families of quintessential avian predators.

BUT THERE WAS ANOTHER elemental linkage as well. Our hawk owl, in a primordial flashback, had linked us to our own primordial past. For the briefest of moments in the charred forest south of Churchill we were all together again as we had been in the beginning. No telephones, no computers, no hum of traffic, no urgency for the next deal. Just fire and water, beak and talon. Just blood and bone, the wind and the sea. Hawk owl news.

A merlin passed us on the trail out. A merlin screaming. The bears were finished denning and were migrating north to the bay. Merlin news. It used to be like this. Conjure and imagine. Where hawk owls prey and merlins scream, it still is.

During years of normal rodent densities, the Hawk Owl winters in the far north, but when vole numbers crash, usually every three to five years, irruptions occur and many birds disperse southward. The majority of the birds involved in these southward irruptions are juveniles.

Chapter Sixteen
Flammulated Owl

The Flammulated Owl is the second smallest, insectivorous, and most migratory owl in North America. It is believed to completely leave for Central America in the winter. It is quickly recognized with its completely dark brown eyes that are not found in any other small owl. The sexes are alike in appearance, although the male and female can be distinguished by call (the female has a higher-pitched, whining call). Their color varies from gray and brown to cinnamon-brown.

The Flam and the Bear

FAR OUT ALONG the peripheries of our consciousness, the splashing in the night-black creekbed became louder, closer, and more insistent. But it was still unnoticed, unheard, and unheeded. Before us, somewhere, from one of the ring of huge ponderosa pines, came the soft, ventriloquial, two-syllabled hoot of the long-imagined, imminently-awaited Flammulated Owl. *"Boo-BOOT."*

Two syllabled! A close encounter, for in a typical sighting (hearing) and on most tapes, only one syllable is audible. Slowly our spotlight probed the shadows created by the full moon, penetrating to the boles of the pines. *"Boo-BOOT."*

Seemingly right before us, then farther off toward the creek, then higher up the slope? We had had this same conversation with a Flam before — several times — in the Pend Oreilles of Washington, in the Blue Range of Oregon, and in the Bradshaws north of Phoenix. Always anticipated, never expected. Exciting, exhilarating, and ultimately frustrating. *"Boo-BOOT."*

The Flammulated Owl is of the genus Otus *with the Screech-Owls, but its ear tufts are smaller than in the Screech-Owls, and it is smaller with longer and pointier wings.*

Flammulated — "flame-colored." Enough rich rufous highlights in the facial disc and along the scapulars to blend perfectly (maddeningly) into the reddish interstices of the ponderosa bark. And our only small North American owl species with dark eyes, absorbing rather than reflecting the searching light. *"Boo-BOOT."*

Very small. Only six inches. Merely the size of a sparrow and, in the illogic of vernacular bird names that so often amuse the non-birder, the Flam is smaller than the pygmy-owls. The Flammulated is a highly-migratory summer resident of our high western mountains, typically found above 5,000 feet in pine/oak associations. It is typically more plentiful in wet weather cycles than in dry. It is also typically difficult to see well, or even to find despite recent surveys showing this elusive forest wraith to be more common than previously thought. *"Boo-BOOT."*

Flammulated Owl

The Flammulated was our ultimate North American owl, the last of the nineteen species. To call it our nemesis was an understatement. The standing family joke was that this species did not really exist, was simply a colossal charade perpetrated on amateur birders by professional ornithologists. Prior to this chilly June night deep in the Chiricahua Mountains of southeastern Arizona, we had never been close enough to hear both syllables. *"Boo-BOOT."* Flam exists!

Here. There. Down by the creek again. Where? Where! Was the bird moving around? Was it sitting tight next to the bole, simply turning its head, projecting the vocalizations in different directions? What was it the literature had said — closer than it sounded, lower than it sounded? Perching only six to ten feet off the ground, the flam darts out to catch night-flying insects, typically beetles, in its talons. Half an hour had passed since the first audible. How long would it hang for us? *"Boo-BOOT."*

Suddenly, finally, the increasingly-obvious commotion emanating from the creekside penetrated the wall of our owl intensive obliviousness. We glanced at each other in simultaneous awareness and disbelief. Recognition, chagrin, and alarm flowed in rapid sequence. Bear!

We were just below the Rustler Park campground. Ranger reports at the visitors' center told of marauding bears prowling the campground at night wreaking havoc on cars and ice chests. We whirled toward the creek, desperately probing the darkness beneath the pine canopy, bumping into one another, cursing softly, giggling silently, light beam splaying about, owl forgotten in the rush of bear adrenaline. No bear to be seen, but the unmistakable rhythm of displaced water surely marking the approach of something very large, surely coming our way. Our van, side-door beckoningly wide open, was fifty yards away, silhouetted in moonlight. "Splash!" The hair on the back of my neck stood tall. Despite all warnings to the contrary, I optimistically knew we could outrun a bear for fifty yards. It was time to move! *"Boo-BOOT."*

The Flam was still there! Wait! We hadn't seen the owl

The Flammulated Owl is almost exclusively an insecti-vore, with their diet including moths, beetles, crickets, grasshoppers, caterpillars, centipedes, millipedes, spiders, and scorpions. Their prey may be taken on the ground, among foliage, and often in the air.

yet! The reiteration of this fact and the absurdity of prioritizing it at this moment sent us into a spasm of nervous activity. Back to back, arms locked, we began a weird, slow, revolving dance toward the van, searchlight mak-ing 360s, first toward the boughs hoping for a chance pass of the Flam through the beam, then toward the stream praying for the beam to intercept nothing from that quarter. The hope and the prayer, the pull of the owl, the push of the bear. *"Boo-BOOT."* *"SPLASH!"*

It took us a while, but we made it without falling, finally collapsing in a heap of uncon-trolled laughter into the door of the van. No owl. No bear. Another miss, this a near and cer-tainly memorable one. Forty miles long, twenty miles wide, a pine clad "sky island" amidst the southeastern grasslands, the Chiricahuas probably combined the highest concentrations of Flams, birders, and bears in Arizona on any given summer night. We saw a bear the next day, ambling down the grade toward South Fork in the broad daylight of mid-morning, acting like nothing so much as king-of-the-road. He saw us too. We were sure he was grinning. We were not to see a Flammulated Owl for another year.

IT WAS IN JULY OF THE following summer in the Bradshaws, 10 p.m., the pines dripping from the passage of a crackling mon-soon thunderstorm. Large green beetles with striking cream antennae were pinging off our camp lantern, shadows of wind-

The Flammulated Owl is generally associated with forests of aspen, ponderosa, and Jeffrey pines where the summers are dry and warm, and where there are available nesting cavities. They may also be found in forests with mixes of oak, Douglas fir, white fir, incense cedar, or sugar pine.

whipped branches playing through the light. Without warning, without a thought, one of the shadows became a shape, perfectly intersecting a beetle's flight on silent wings. Flam had found us! Our searchlight picked it out instantly — smaller, lower, closer than imperfectly imagined over all the years — watching from a horizontal bough, plying its trade in the cool, damp mountain darkness, stalking the bizarre bugs attracted to our light.

We exchanged a muted high five, bantered softly about the bird's "countability" because of our light's assistance, dismissed the issue with an easy cynicism bred of years of futility, then enjoyed our guest's smooth, mostly successful forays through our campsite. Or were we the guests?

Today we are aware of many sites throughout Arizona and the mountain west where we and others have had Flammulated Owl encounters. Mostly these encounters have been unexpected. New owlers always ask where and when. We always reply with that old aphorism that applies to so many of the very special species on the birder's classic "want list" — always in the right habitat but never when you're looking for it. That's what makes the Flammulated Owl one of those very special species, every search an unbridled adventure.

Flammulated Owl wing from above and below.

Chapter Seventeen

Ferruginous Pygmy-Owl

The Ferruginous Pygmy-Owl's range just barely extends into North America from Central and South America. It is a diurnal owl, although mostly crepuscular (active at dawn and dusk). As its name implies (ferruginous is defined as reddish-brown or rust in color), a major distinctive field mark of this owl is the rufous or reddish-brown tail bars and overall color. It is very similar to the Northern Pygmy-Owl, but is distinct in habitat, call, color, and tail band color.

Guns, Lies, and Videotape

"Ferruginous pygmy-owls belong in Mexico. If you want to see one go down there."

Guess which one of the following people made that statement: a) the governor of Arizona, rebuffing attempts by environmental groups to have land preserved as habitat for this owl; b) a leader for a bird tour company, rebuffing my inquiry about where to look for this owl in Arizona; c) the home owner in Pima County, Arizona, who pulled a gun on me, rebuffing my determination to get a better "life" look at this species as I sat in my vehicle on a public street across from his property glassing a saguaro hole into which an owl had gone to roost.

If you answered "all of the above," you're well on your way to understanding that the Ferruginous Pygmy-Owl is the Southwestern desert's analogue to the Spotted Owl of the Pacific Northwest rain forests, a seven-inch long lightning rod attracting all manner of those with any kind of stake in the desert's devel-

opment or preservation. In the first case, the quote was a direct one made to the newsprint media in the summer of 1999. In the second instance, the quote is a slightly paraphrased version made to me by a birding friend in 1991. In the final scenario, the quote is an expletive-deleted rendering snarled at me just before dawn on May 27, 1985.

My response in 1985, as you may suspect, was "Yes, SIR!" My response to my friend in 1991 was to chide his stonewalling, remind him how much we had birded together, lament how many of our mutual acquaintances in southern Arizona had flat-out lied to me about locations for this bird. When Maricopa (Phoenix) Audubon's conservation officer responded to Governor Hull's remark in 1999 by characterizing her/it as "zany," it made me realize that man's relationship with the owls has changed relatively little since the dawn of the millennium. Here is a story passed down through generations of Apaches:

During a periodic drought a pygmy owl appeared in a dream to a powerful warrior's young bride. The owl told her the rains would come again if she killed her husband and returned his horses to the Spanish, forcing her people to give up their marauding lifestyle and return to the land for sustenance. That night she stabbed the sleeping warrior and rode off into the desert with his herd. Coming to a waterhole which she knew to be dry, she found it overbrimming. When the owl of her dream appeared in a nearby bush and called to her, she became fearful and shot it. It transformed itself into her slain husband who rose up, killed her, collected the horses, and returned to his band to find a more faithful lover. The summer rains came the next day.

THEN AND NOW, both feared and revered, owls and the things they seem to represent have always possessed a spooky, outsized power to make men act in strange ways, believe in strange things, and tell strange tales. Which of these is the stranger? That an educated elder of a state's most highly-respected conservation group would publicly call the highest elected official of that state "zany," or that that official could be so environmentally-challenged she

Ferruginous Pygmy-Owl
Glaucidium brasilianum

Most frequently heard vocalization
Series of rapidly repeated "Hoo" notes, 2-3 per second; higher pitched than Northern Pygmy-Owl

Size
A small owl, 6.75" long with a 12" wingspan; approximately the size of a sparrow

Most notable physical features
• tiny size, no ear tufts
• long tail with broad, reddish bars
• yellow eyes
• plain, rusty back, rusty streaks on sides

Seasonal movement
Permanent resident

Nest sites
Woodpecker holes and natural tree cavities

Habits
Diurnal

Range/habitat
Ferruginous Pygmy-Owls are found in the extreme southern areas of Arizona and southern Texas; it is typically found in wooded river bottoms and saguaro deserts near the Mexican border.

The only overlap of range between the Northern and the Ferruginous Pygmy-Owls is in a very small area of southern Arizona, so the possibility of mistaking their identification is slight. Additionally, the Ferruginous is a lowland bird while the Northern Pygmy is a mountain bird.

would not appreciate the "development" of both the saguaro deserts of Arizona and the thorn scrub forests of northern Mexico as a microcosm of a vast global disease?

A month after accosting me across from his property in Pima County, enraged by tour vans working his street at strange hours, the home owner with the gun blew away the owl in question with his gun. Or so the story goes. Which is zanier, the killing if in fact it happened, or the rumor, started by the birding powers-that-be so that the killing would not happen? The mystique of the tiny desert pygmy-owl, working its zany magic upon the land and its people — timeless.

ON MAY 12, 1971, in a stand of large cottonwoods at Blue Point on the north bank of the Salt River, Roy Johnson, an owl researcher, saw the last confirmed Ferruginous Pygmy-Owl in Maricopa County, Arizona. There was no one there to corroborate his sighting. On June 26, 1999, my wife, our two sons, their wives and their three children floated past the Blue Point cottonwoods in two canoes. There were no pygmy owls there to sight us. There were 115 people, 95 innertubes, 56 empty beer cans, and two competing boom boxes, the loudest blaring out the 1970 rock classic, *American Woman*. The ghetto scene decried by The Guess Who had indeed found its way into this once-pristine desert setting. A week later, over the July 4th holiday weekend, Tonto National Forest personnel logged 100,000(!) "recreationists"

Ferruginous Pygmy-Owl

(read "drunken revelers") through the Blue Point area on the Salt.

In the early 1900s, the Ferruginous Pygmy-Owl was common in Arizona from the Salt-Verde confluence south to the Mexican border, from the Cabeza Prieta desert east to the town of Safford. It now occupies ten percent of its former range north of Mexico, in Arizona and Texas. In Arizona that former range was deciduous riparian, primarily cottonwood, bordered by mature mesquite bosques. In Arizona, only ten percent of that historic riparian habitat survives. The reasons are primarily livestock grazing, woodcutting, water table depletion, and urban encroachment, certainly a litany of the causes of our global disease.

T HE DESERT PYGMY-OWL favors woodpecker holes for nesting and the desert woodpecker of Arizona, the gila, cannot excavate hardwood such as mesquite. With the cottonwoods all but gone and those that are left segregated from the mesquite, the Ferruginous Pygmy-Owl has been virtually extirpated from Arizona.

In Texas, where the owls' range is not cottonwood but oak and ebony bordered by mesquite, the resident woodpecker is the golden-fronted, a more salutary ally since this woodpecker can excavate hardwood. Texas' pygmies utilize nestholes primarily in the live oak stands, and are faring better than Arizona's.

In Texas, if a birder sees a Ferruginous Pygmy-Owl, it is in the lower Rio Grande Valley below Falcon Dam or on one of the

In Arizona, the Ferruginous Pygmy-Owl occurs in saguaro desert, mesquite, and cottonwood-mesquite habitats. In Texas, it is now mostly confined to remaining patches of mesquite, ebony, and cane along the lower Rio Grande River.

The Ferruginous Pygmy-Owl is a diurnal and crepuscular owl feeding mostly on insects such as grasshoppers, crickets, caterpillars, other large insects and scorpions. In addition, their diet consists of birds, small mammals, amphibians, and reptiles (often lizards).

huge, undeveloped ranches in Kenedy County. In Arizona, if a birder sees one (a vanishingly-small likelihood since there have been only twenty officially-confirmed sightings since 1970), no one ever hears about it. Lying about Ferruginous Pygmy-Owl sightings has become a point of honor among Arizona birders.

During the late 1980s I spent many hours "practice bleeding," tramping around the historic hot spot in the grazed-out desert where the Salt and Verde conjoin northeast of Phoenix, looking for Ferruginous Pygmy-Owls. Of course I never saw one, but no other birders in the state were seeing any by then either… or at least they weren't reporting them. Maybe they should have been. In May of 1992 Peter Galvin of the Gila Biodiversity Project petitioned to have the Ferruginous Pygmy-Owl listed as a Federally Endangered Species. It was a hard sell. If there were no owls out there… He could not get the government's attention. No action was taken.

In the fall of 1993 a Tucson homeowner whose property abutted a large wash heard what she later described as a "bleeping" sound in her backyard. She discovered a pygmy-owl, video-taped it, and after several inquiries discovered what a miraculously-rare visitor she had. Not an active birder and unburdened by the hard core birder's emotional and political dilemma regarding the reporting of rare owls, she alerted state wildlife authorities. She named her owl "Bleepy."

Bleepy's discovery in a quiet, sparsely-developed section of Tucson's desert which was then poised on the brink of a building boom "opened the ball." There *were* owls out there! The federal government belatedly and begrudgingly became involved in the joys and wonders of the desert pygmy.

Eventually, in December of 1998, after surveys by the now venerable Roy Johnson, Secretary of State Bruce Babbitt officially declared the Ferruginous Pygmy-Owl endangered. Arizona Game & Fish, following Babbitt's initiative, designated 750,000 acres in Pima and Pinal counties as critical Ferruginous Pygmy-Owl habitat. A Baptist church and a new high school were the largest of 53 planned construction projects put on hold. A spokeswoman for the largest home developer in the state, incensed about the surveys, complained that Game & Fish had "too much time on their hands" and asked this question: "Can't the owls just fly away when the bulldozers approach their territory?" Zany. Bleepy's legacy.

Like the Northern Pygmy-Owl, the Ferruginous is a bold and ferocious daytime predator, sometimes attacking prey larger than itself, such as American Robins or young domestic fowl.

In August of 1996, amidst the ongoing angst of birders hoping to see one of the owls and developers hoping they would not, yet another homeowner abutting another wash discovered a pair of owls frequenting her birdbath in the broad light of day. She too videotaped them. A very keen but relatively new-to-Arizona-birding-politics observer saw the tapes, excitedly confirmed the sighting and then inexplicably put it out there before God and everyone on the Tucson hotline. Neither of these owls was Bleepy, but birders and developers alike spewed forth a lot of rhetoric with "bleep" in every sentence.

The Ferruginous Pygmy-Owl is endangered in Arizona and facing loss of habitat in both Texas and Arizona. It is still quite frequent over much of its Mexican range.

Seven times I have hiked the rutted road down below Falcon Dam in the Rio Grande Valley of Texas looking for a Ferruginous Pygmy-Owl. To no avail. This compares favorably with the fourteen trips my friend from Austin has made to no avail. I have seen a Ferruginous three times in Arizona. The first was at gunpoint in May of 1985. I won't lie to you about my most recent sighting — like many others, carrying all my emotional and political owl baggage, I searched the wash and found one of the August, 1996 birds.

In between, in August of 1987, I had my most satisfying Ferruginous Pygmy-Owl encounter. Most satisfying because there were no guns and no guilt involved. No obfuscation. No recrimination. No phony directions or raised eyebrows. I stumbled upon one myself. I won't lie to you about this one either. It was at the intersection of two canyons, Booger and Hell Hole. If you can find that spot on Arizona topos, if you can get yourself to that spot, if the owls are still there and vocalizing and you can find one, then you deserve a check by Ferruginous Pygmy-Owl on your life list.

I know an avid Arizona birder who claims the desert pygmy-owl on his life list. He has excellent videotaped footage that he has shown to other birders. Discreet inquiries are met with averted eyes and evasive answers. He steadfastly disclaims seeing it in his home state or including it on his state list. But I know he has never birded Texas nor ever set foot in Mexico. Strange that a seven-inch bird has the power to evoke such passion and allegiance. Strange that an intelligent species has not yet translated that passion and allegiance into saving its own planet.

Look in the mirror and repeat after me. *Mea culpa.*

Above: Both pygmy-owls have "false eyes," a distinctive pair of black patches bordered with white on the nape. Right: Ferruginous Pygmy-Owls are cavity nesters.

Chapter Eighteen
Boreal Owl

The Boreal Owl is a nocturnal owl that lives in the northern boreal forests around the world. It is of the same genus as the Northern Saw-whet Owl, and while the two are similar in appearance, the Boreal Owl is larger and generally deep brown in contrast to the Saw-whet's reddish-brown back and chestnut streaking. The Boreal's crown is thickly white spotted with larger white markings on the back also. The male and female are alike in plumage.

Shadows Across the Meadow

ESCUDILLA. The name resonates mellifluously on the tongue and settles seamlessly into the crannies and crevices of any mind that in downtime conjures last great places — places to go before it is too late — and considers great last places — places to be after it is too late.

Escudilla Mountain, Arizona's third highest at 10,876, is a remote, brooding hulk rising above the national forests that mantle the east-central portion of this "desert" state. Not peaked but a flat-topped plateau half-a-day across by horseback, Escudilla is a remnant bowl of some ancient, blown volcano. Inaccessible beneath blankets of snow in wet winters and wracked by violent thunderstorms in wet summers, Escudilla is a vast expanse of spruce/fir habitat interspersed with glades of aspen, wet meadow, and rimrock. If Escudilla did not exist in the physical realm, it would be fabricated by the imaginations of outdoor enthusiasts seeking a visual depiction of what "wilderness" verbally implies.

The Boreal Owl inhabits the northern coniferous and mixed deciduous boreal and subalpine forests of North America.

Some oral histories suggest that "Escudilla" is the anglicized version of "the lost ones." Aldo Leopold, the timber cruiser/forest ranger who rode the Apache-Sitgreaves in the early years of the twentieth century and later eulogized the mountain in his classic wilderness paean, *A Sand County Almanac*, would be pleased with this notion, not that he spent any time seeking the range cattle that inevitably disappeared into the rugged mountain's hidden draws and steep ravines, but because he experienced first hand on Escudilla the demise of the two most requisite and revered wilderness components — grizzly bear and wolf.

Leopold, certainly himself not blameless, indicated in his essays and journals that well before his death in 1948 he had come to full awareness that losses such as these, irrevocable as they then seemed, diminished our country's wellness, its wholeness, eliminating the "wild" from our wilderness. He writes regretfully of the "fierce green fire dying" in the eye of the she-wolf he and fellow rangers had gunned down in youthful trigger itch. Wistfully he alludes to the death of Bigfoot, the last of Arizona's grizzlies, killed on Escudilla by a set gun rigged by a government trapper in the 1930s.

By the mid-1980s we had camped and explored Escudilla. We had glassed its Wild Turkeys from behind a springtime blowdown; we had rolled in its summer wildflowers; we had hiked its groves of glittering autumn aspen. We had read *A Sand County Almanac* too, and realized a far more important wilderness conundrum than tree-falling-in-uninhabited-woods. Is it wilderness if man is there but he doesn't hear the howling of the unseen pack nor ever sees the huge pawprint in creekside gravel? Is it wilderness if the scenes in one's mind are unmatched by the experiences of one's five senses? Is it wilderness if the imagination lies fallow, unfertilized by the surge of adrenaline up the spine and along the base of the scalp?

ALL THAT CHANGED for Escudilla in the spring of 1987. In April of that year Boreal Owls were discovered along Dixie Creek in Rio Arriba County, New Mexico. These were not random, transient birds escaping the rigors of a far northern winter, but breeding Boreal Owls. Aldo Leopold, apparently not a "birder" in any latter day sense of that term, does not tell us if Boreal Owls, the quintessential wilderness owl, were present on Escudilla during his rambles there. But Bureau of Land Management (BLM) researcher Tom Gatz proposed logically and convincingly that if a relict population of Boreals was living in northern New Mexico, the possibilities for Arizona were very real. He reported Boreal bones found in prehistoric cave deposits in southern New Mexico; he catalogued remnant pockets of the preferred spruce/fir habitat in Arizona; and he pinpointed three areas most worthy of the search — Green's Peak, Mt. Baldy, and Escudilla.

Green's Peak is a small and isolated cinder cone, steep on top and buffeted incessantly by nasty winds that have scoured its south and west faces and left them treeless. The

Boreal Owl
Aegolius funereus

Most frequently heard vocalization
Series of rapidly repeated, low, short whistled toots; high-pitched and very resonant

Size
A medium-sized owl, 10" long with a 21" wingspan; about the size of a Robin

Most notable physical features
• large head
• white face with distinctive black border
• yellow eyes
• long-winged and long-tailed
• chocolate streaking on underparts

Seasonal movement
Sedentary, but irruptive movement southward in winter by young birds into northern tier of the U.S. as prey species periodically fluctuate

Nest sites
Woodpecker holes, natural tree cavities; will use nest boxes

Habits
Nocturnal

Range/habitat
Boreal Owls are found in conifer forests and tamarack bogs across Alaska, Canada, and south through the highest parts of the Rocky Mountains.

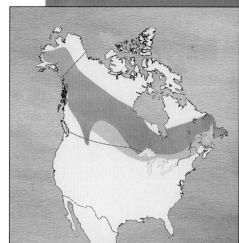

spruce/fir areas on the peak's north and east exposures are tangled and trailless. Baldy, its apex much larger, completely forested, and accessible by two well-used trails, would be a better candidate were it not that the peak itself lies on Native American land — sacred ground. Hikers straying beyond ill-defined boundaries have been accosted and arrested.

Escudilla. Out from the closets of the mind, special again in a very real sense, it took only the suspicion, the thought, of a species such as Boreal Owl for Leopold's beloved "on top" to revert to some nineteenth century level of wholeness, despite the absence of grizzly and wolf. Anyone who has ever heard the winnowing springtime call of the Boreal Owl, startingly strong, resonant and haunting for such a small owl, echoing through dark and silent chambers of spruce and fir, knows well the meaning of "forest primeval" and the jangle of adrenaline across spine and scalp. Eagerly we took notes on Tom's articles and poured over Escudilla's topo maps.

BOREAL IN ITS most literal sense refers to the three most northerly life zones on the continent; Arctic, Hudsonian, and Canadian. In a more visceral sense, boreal refers to that great white north of ice, snow, and coniferous forest largely uninhabited by man, and only sparsely inhabited by creatures we encounter in print but never in real life (creatures we can only hope someday to actually see). Boreal Owl is certainly one of those creatures, mysterious and seldom seen, formerly called Richardson's Owl after the Scottish adventurer/naturalist who first described it (and fittingly, the grizzly also once bore his name —Richardson's Barren Ground Grizzly).

As recently as the early 1970s, the Boreal Owl was unknown as a breeder in the lower forty-eight. Birders here had three choices: they could gaze at the Boreal's seemingly surreal depiction in a field guide and dream; they could wait for the sporadic winter irruption of Boreals around the Great Lakes or in upper New England; or they could stand next to Bob Dittrick hoping upraised eyebrows of the inquisitive-appearing

Boreal's facial disk would appear as Bob scratched on one of his research nesting boxes outside of Anchorage.

The concept of life zones held the key to the Boreals' discovery in the high Rockies. Proper habitat near Anchorage occurs at 2,000 feet. The same mix of Engelmann spruce, lodgepole pine, Douglas fir, and ponderosa pine occurs farther south, but at increasingly higher elevations — between 5,500 and 9,000 feet in the northernmost tier of states, and from 9,000 to 11,000 in the southern Rockies. Neither owls nor habitat had undergone sudden and dramatic range expansion. Both had been there for eons, the owls going undetected mainly for two reasons. Spruce/fir has had little economic value to loggers. Spruce/fir during early spring, the most vocal time in the boreals' life cycle, is damn cold and inaccessible to all but the most intrepid birders.

Boreal Owls usually hunt by perching on low branches or tree trunks. The owl will scan the ground by moving its head slowly from side to side, listening for movement of potential prey, as they hunt primarily using their excellent, directional hearing. Prey items are mainly small rodents, especially voles.

SEMI-INTREPID, WE had chosen late October, 1988. It was Saturday, midnight. Clear and cold. Moon waxing full. We started again up Escudilla, paralleling Paddy Creek to the Halsey Lake cutoff. Tonight instead of taking the trail from Halsey to the top, we planned to follow Paddy Fork to Toolbox Draw, then survey around the meadows and cienegas of Terry Flat to Punchbowl Spring. The previous night's attempt, hindered by clouds and a howling wind, had produced no owls and no responses.

Though Boreals will respond differently in fall than in spring, the drill is the same in both seasons. Find spruce/fir above 9,000 feet, the higher the better, interspersed with meadow. Play the

Boreal Owl

staccato call of the male owl every half mile, standing back in the trees off the meadow's edge with observers facing different directions. Play the tape for at least five minutes, starting very loud, then gradually decreasing the volume to barely audible. Watch for movement through the trees or shadows across the meadow. Listen for wings slapping against branches. Listen to your heart pulsing wildly in your ears as your hyper-alert senses sort through every nuance of the night. Bob Dittrick will produce owls, but he will not produce this rush.

In early spring the hope is to hear the staccato call, though not necessarily in response to the tape. If Boreals respond at all in the fall, it will not be with this "primary" call, but with *SKIEW* or *OO-WORK*, both short, sharp contact calls. Know that Boreals may come to investigate in the fall without making any response. Know that Boreals may come, undetected, to within ten feet. Know that Saw-whet Owls inhabit Boreal territory, give a similar *SKIEW* call, and are superficially similar in less than optimal lighting conditions.

BY 2 A.M. WE WERE at 10,500 feet working our way downhill below Profanity Ridge, shivering, sleepwalking, negotiating how much longer to press on. Heat, not warming either of us, radiated from Deva's voice as she declared this her last stop. Dutifully I dialed down the volume and clicked off the tape player. At that very moment from the aspen grove before us came a single, sharp, unmistakable *SKIEW*, instantly firing the blood, fueling the senses, and rendering thoughts of sleeping bags irrelevant.

It would be all too perfect to report that we turned our searchbeam directly onto a Boreal peering down at us in rapt inquisitivity. But birding is not always like that and owling certainly is not. An hour's intense and desperate search in

A Boreal Owl can locate and capture prey strictly audibly, such as beneath the snow or vegetation. It will also cache food and can later thaw it if necessary by performing brooding-like behavior over it.

widening circles from the *SKIEW* epicenter produced nothing more interesting than an etching in the bark of the largest aspen I had ever seen, which read: "Humpy Walker 8 - __81." And the enscabbed and obscured numbers in front of the 81 looked more like 18 than 19! I vowed in my next life to return to Escudilla not as an owl researcher but as a cultural historian.

Over a late breakfast campfire the next morning we obsessed over what we could have done differently, how we might reconstruct the scenario to supply needed answers to haunting questions. With only one snatch of vocalization and without any visual verification, we could get no farther than this: we had heard something in the woods last night, possibly a Saw-whet Owl, and we would relish the delicious prospect of returning again and often to the tantalizing search for the unseen and least-known of the owls. Escudilla has never given up its lost ones easily.

Boreal Owls nest mainly in old woodpecker cavities, but will also use natural cavities. They take readily to artificial nest boxes.

A S I PEN THIS epilogue to our most recent visit to Escudilla, my subconscious picks up the Beatles playing in the background: *As I write this letter, send my love to you…* I am abashed. I have never written to a mountain before, but a momentous change has taken place. No one has found Boreal owls there, but Mexican gray wolves have been reintroduced, released in March of 1998 into the Blue Primitive Area just to the south and virtually in Escudilla's shadow! If not there already, they will find Escudilla soon enough, lost ones homing to their natural wilderness niche. Aldo Leopold would be surprised and ecstatic. And some romantic eco-biologist, roaming far ahead of his pack, has already uttered the "G" word, making the once unlikely at least thinkable. Bigfoot's genetic ancestors may wander Escudilla's glades and meadows to raise the hackles and lift the imaginations of our grandchildren.

M̲Y LIFE, TOO, HAS changed in oh-so-many ways. My beloved wife of thirty-five years, working through the tangled web of menopause, seems but a stranger to me on certain days. But that is the least. She has placed her able-bodied father in an Alzheimer's home and I have buried my mother, unrequited and estranged to the very end of her long and lonely dance with cancer. Our oldest son has endured an acrimonious divorce, our youngest a traumatic separation. One ex-spouse, diagnosed with obsessive-compulsive disorder and on medication to regulate her brain chemistry, has been awarded custody of our two oldest grandchildren. The other ex has gone to see a cosmetic surgeon, then run off to become an exotic dancer, leaving our youngest grandchild behind. As Dave Barry always reiterates at the end of his most outrageous scenarios, I am not making this up.

It is early spring. Time has come today. In the farthest recesses of my mind a latch has turned, a long-secured hatch sprung open. Long ago and far away I grasped the meaning of wilderness. I have a full tank of gas and fifty rolls of Provia. I have my warmest sleeping bag. I have my snowshoes. The wolves are back. There may be Boreals on top. I may come upon the huge pawprint in the snow, bloody elk carcass with pulverized skull nearby. I may disappear into wilderness news — ashes to ashes across the ancient cinder cone.

Escudilla.

Boreal Owls live to be about seven or eight years old. Incubating females are sometimes killed by Pine Martens. They are also preyed upon by larger raptors, such as other owls and Goshawks.

Chapter Nineteen
Great Gray Owl

One of the world's largest owls, the Great Gray Owl is dark grey overall interspersed with bars and flecks of light grey and white. Its Latin name, "nebulosa" is derived from the Latin "Nebulosus," meaning misty or foggy. The Great Gray Owl has also been commonly called Great Gray Ghost, Phantom of the North, Spectral Owl, and Bearded Owl.

Whispers of the Night

THE GHOSTLY GRAY SPECTER slipped from the forest vastness behind my right shoulder, across my peripheral vision, and out over the dew-drenched, moonlit meadow, floating just above the ground like some ethereal wraith. Disbelieving, I grabbed Deva's arm and squeezed, hard, pointing toward the phantom form through a pulsing surge of adrenaline.

At the far edge of the meadow, the apparition swept abruptly upwards, as owls will do, alighting atop a four-foot snag. Click! No light. No time for a tripod. No time to quell the trembling, quaking like one of the nearby aspen. But my mind's lens captured the scene in perfect, crystalline focus, the forever essence of a lifetime of owl-search. Chevron Meadow, Yosemite National Park.

The first flash on my mindscreen was of old Dick Davenport, lying in the Yosemite grass, perhaps this same meadow, several autumns ago, dying as he fingered his cable release. Those who are both birding enthusiasts and long-faithful followers of Garry

These two juvenile Great Gray Owls are waiting for a parent to return with food. Next page: The Great Gray Owl is a ponderous flier, does not often move more than short distances between perches, and seldom glides. They fly close to the ground, usually less than 20 feet up, except when flying to a nest.

Trudeau's comic strip, *Doonesbury*, will never forget the fateful date, November 6, 1986. On that day, Dick simultaneously achieved mortality and instant immortality, clicking his camera shutter on a suspected-to-be-extinct Bachman's warbler, even as he breathed his last breath in the throes of a massive coronary resulting from the accompanying adrenaline surge. I do not know if Trudeau is a birder but, if not, he must know someone who is, for his take on the whole scenario was spot on.

Luckily my arteries were not diseased. Luckily Deva was experiencing the same adrenaline surge, not feeling the strength of mine against her arm. That evening we discovered the perfect imprint of my five fingers on her biceps, already discoloring to purples and blacks, perhaps like the taloned grip but certainly without the incisor sharpness with which the Great Gray Owl dispatches the meadow voles and other small mammals that predominate its prey preference.

GREAT GRAY IS ONE of four owls included in Mlodinow and O'Brien's *America's 100 Most Wanted Birds*, and certainly it is near the top of most birders' much shorter "short list." It was not, for us, the most frustratingly elusive of the owl family (Flammulated), nor was it the species for which we had traveled the farthest (Northern Hawk), spent the most time searching (Ferruginous), or prioritized back when it all began (Snowy). But it was very near the ultimate in all those categories, and the Yosemite setting in which we finally scored *Strix nebulosa* was the quintessential owl paradigm for this aptly-named North American owl.

The dark, silent, and deserted mountain meadow was surrounded by nebulous silhouettes of ancient trees filtering a limning moonlight that cast every branch and bush into surreal uncertainty. We felt every baited anticipation without any shred of rational expectation. The movement, disbelieved when suddenly discerned, exploded upon our hyper-alert senses, a visual orgasm damping breath and speech and even thought. The owl had come. Yes! It was enough. Nothing else in any real world mattered for that moment. A Dick Davenport moment.

WE HAVE FOUND the easiest way to bring non-birding friends to an understanding of what all the fuss is about is allusion to collecting or hunting. We are accumulating bird sightings, bird experiences, in much the same manner and with many of the same emotions as those who collect fine art or sports memorabilia. We are hunting non-consumptively with binoculars and camera rather than gun or bow. And Great Gray Owl is the dust-laden, cobweb-festooned masterpiece chanced upon in some back corner of some tawdry antique emporium, the trophy bull tracked exhaustingly through miles of knee-deep snow across the inclines of some untraced mountain wilderness.

Great Gray Owl
Strix nebulosa

Most frequently heard vocalization
Series of very deep, muffled, pumping "Hoo" notes, slightly lower at end

Size
A large owl, 30" long with a 52" wingspan; about the size of a hawk

Most notable physical features
• large size with disproportionately large head
• concentric dark circles on facial disk make yellow eyes appear small
• black-and-white "bow tie" on throat
• long tail

Seasonal movement
Irruptive movement southward in winter into northern tier of U.S. as prey species fluctuate

Nest sites
Stick platforms, broken top snags; will use artificial nest platforms

Habits
Diurnal

Range/habitat
Great Gray Owls are found in conifer forests with bogs and meadows across Canada and Alaska and into the northern Rocky Mountains and upper Great Lakes.

Great Gray Owl

Like the lost masterpiece or the ten-point buck, the value of the bird to the birder increases with its scarcity, its elusiveness, the lengths physical, temporal, and financial to which the seeker must go to secure it, and the mindset with which the seeker seeks. The quester after Great Grays is perforce a wilderness romantic. The quester of the Great Gray would like, if only for an hour or a day, to *be* a Great Gray, to fly in solitude the antediluvian forests and bogs where everyday life cannot intrude, feel for an instant a life that everyday people cannot imagine.

The Great Gray is huge by owl standards, our largest owl by size though not by body weight. It is all head and wings — blunt, rounded, tuftless head and long slabs of wings with wide blades of feathers. It is elusive, not by design, but by virtue of large territories set in tracts of outback and bush that seekers seldom access, its populations dependent upon cycles of rodent prey over which man has no control and little understanding. It is not often vocal, but those vocalizations are hauntingly deep and resonant. It hunts by dark, but is often active at dawn and dusk when its cryptic gray plumage mimes the shadows and mocks the whispers of the night. The Great Gray is truly the owl collector's ultimate item.

When perched, Great Gray Owls appear very bulky because of their dense, fluffy plumage, long wings that extend past the body, relatively long tail, and a large head. Their feet are heavily feathered but remain hidden from view when perched.

PRIOR TO THIS SEANCE in Chevron Meadow we had spent the better part of four vacations on great gray owl quest, chasing rumors, seeing not the owl but experiencing wild and beautiful country that the owl surely haunted. We had beaten and sloshed our way through Minnesota's legendary Sax-Zim bog in head nets, ending each day with a thorough tick inspection. We had traversed Yellowstone Canyon's pocket meadows in prelude-to-dawn blackness, whirling in frenzied grizzly fear at every slightest

sound. We had hiked northeast Washington's Pend Oreille, thoroughly lost in a maze of game trails after detouring from mother moose with calf. And our first foray into Yosemite had been summarily terminated by forest fire.

"Exposures" seems a more fitting word than "experiences." Fire and water, small beasts that suck blood, large beasts that can eviscerate — that is Great Gray Owl territory, unforgiving and, like the great owl itself, unpredictable. It is country assigned some forgotten niche deep within our genetic coding, country well known to our forebears but not nearly well enough known to enough of us today.

Here are two of the more compelling reasons we collectors quest the rarer owls. It takes us places from whence we, as a species, have come, and it proves that we, as a species, are not the center of this universe. Both are messages many of our species do not understand or, understanding all too well, relegate into denial.

We should not, cannot, ignore or deny this terrain on our genetic map. In a time and culture where *having* has taken precedence over *being*, we need exposure to these places that recall to us who we were, instruct us as to who we are, and counsel us on who we should become. And for those without physical access, the knowledge alone of these places lends shape to a spiritual terrain that will cultivate living rather than consuming.

The Great Gray Owl may not prove there is something out there greater than ourselves, but it surely proves there is something out there over which we have no control. We enter this terrain, whether hiking its trails or plumbing our souls, on *its* terms. The owl stalks its prey, copulates, protects its branchers, breaks a wing, starves and dies, all untended in the unknown. Man once did these same things, in like conditions, over the same terrain. The owl knows the territory, evokes the time, reminds us we were there. And it is these reminders, genetic mementos, that have drawn us, drawn Native Americans, drawn the first generation which picked its knuckles from the ground, to the palpable mystery and intrigue, to the imagined sagacity and clairvoyance, of the owl tribes.

Opposite: Male and female Great Grey Owls will aggressively defend nests and have been known to drive off predators as large as black bears. Among other threats, ravens and Great Horned Owls prey on eggs and nestlings. Below: The Great Grey Owl has a distinctive primary call, which is a very soft, low-pitched hoot "whooo-ooo-ooo-ooo" with the notes emitted slowly over a six- to eight-second period. Calls are repeated every 15-30 seconds. This call is used as a territorial declaration and can be heard up to a half-mile away.

THE GREAT GRAY, across the meadow through the mists of time, had stretched, preened, and conjured up first light. Now it flew, low and languidly, into the primeval, untended cathedral forests. We watched it out of sight, lingered, then turned, emotionally drained, back toward the road, reluctant as always to leave the site of such a long-sought spectacle that might never be revisited.

It was no mystery why this fifth journey specifically for Great Gray had been successful. Our youngest son, now a professional river guide, had visited us before we left, himself on his way to his first run by raft through

The very large head with prominent gray concentric circles on the facial disk make this owl's eyes appear small.

the Grand Canyon. It was he who had held the Great Horned Owl carcass in the Cascades those many years before, held the book on owls while we parsed the text of evolution. It was he who had plucked the serrated primary. On this visit, he had returned that talisman to us, woven by a craftsman friend into a dream catcher, now adorning our van's rear view mirror.

Halfway to the van, in a flash of realization, I wheeled and ran the path back to the meadow, wishfully thinking the great owl might have returned. It had not of course, but there beneath its snag, still morning damp with dew, was a single speckled gray blade from the great wing. As I had known it would be.

Hiking out I reflected on Yosemite and Dick Davenport, his perfect death. From there the thread led to my friend Dan who wished to take his terminal walk into the wild canyons of the

Great Gray Owl

Paria, all the better if owls be there; then to my mother who had danced her last long and lonely dance with breast cancer escorted by a screech owl. And Devin and JP, exposed to fledgling city owls, hopefully exposed to a lifetime pilgrimage through a natural world that has much to teach them about that lifetime.

Throughout recorded history owls have been a link, a bridge — day to night, life to death, what man knows and what he can see to what he might not want to know and what he can only imagine — present to past, now to then, shadows between the illumination and the void. Understanding is The Grail, the pilgrimage not yet completed, not ever completed, owl-sign at every point along the trail. Some say priest. Some say sorcerer.

Strix nebulosa. I wove the Great Gray Owl primary into the dream catcher, weaving dreams of summers yet unknown, summers of dreams yet unfulfilled. Alaska's Wrangell-St. Elias. Oregon's Blue Range. Minnesota's Gunflint Trail. Good places for Great Grays. Good places to be. Like Escudilla, not bad places to die. Places to terminate an unfinished journey.

The Great Gray Owl thermo-regulates by roosting in dense cover. When hot, a Great Gray Owl will pant and droop its wings to expose an unfeathered area under the wing.

Photo Credits

Page 2 © Robert McCaw
Page 4 © Jim Burns / Natural Impacts
Page 6 © Donald M. Jones
Page 8 © Brian E. Small
Page 9 © Middleton Evans / Folio, Inc.
Page 10 © Gary R. Zahm
Page 11 © Robert McCaw
Page 12 © Lisa & Mike Husar / TeamHusar.com
Page 14 © Jim Burns / Natural Impacts
Page 15 © Lynn M. Stone
Page 16 © Michael Fairchild / Peter Arnold, Inc.
Page 18-19 © Middleton Evans / Folio, Inc.
Page 20 © Cas Sowa
Page 21 © Jim Burns / Natural Impacts
Page 22 © Brain E. Small
Page 23 © Lisa & Mike Husar / TeamHusar.com
Page 24 © Michael H. Francis / RonKimballStock.com
Page 26 © Erwin & Peggy Bauer
Page 27 © Tom & Pat Leeson
Page 28 © Tom & Pat Leeson
Page 31 © Cas Sowa
Page 32 © Jim Burns / Natural Impacts
Page 33 © Lisa & Mike Husar / TeamHusar.com
Page 34 © Gail Shumway
Page 36 © Jim Burns / Natural Impacts
Page 37 © Donald M. Jones
Page 38 © Donald M. Jones
Page 40 © Brian E. Small
Page 41 © Donald M. Jones
Page 43 © Richard Day / Daybreak Imagery
Page 44 © Jim Burns / Natural Impacts
Page 46 © Donald M. Jones
Page 47 © Tom & Pat Leeson
Page 48 © Michio Hoshino / Minden Pictures
Page 50 © Cheryl Ertelt
Page 51 © David L. Sladky
Page 52 © Gail Shumway
Page 53 © Ken Thommes
Page 54 © Lynn M. Stone
Page 56 © Jim Burns / Natural Impacts
Page 57 © Donald M. Jones
Page 58 © Donald M. Jones
Page 61 © Tim Christie
Page 62 © Lon Lauber / AlaskaStock.com
Page 63 © Donald M. Jones
Page 64 © Jim Burns / Natural Impacts
Page 66 © Jim Burns / Natural Impacts
Page 67 © Richard Day / Daybreak Imagery

Page 68 © Jim Burns / Natural Impacts
Page 71 © Anita Weiner
Page 72 © Steve & Dave Maslowski
Page 73 Top © Joe McDonald
Page 73 Bottom © Mike & Lisa Husar / TeamHusar.com
Page 74 © Robert McCaw
Page 76 © Brian E. Small
Page 77 © Tim Christie
Page 78 © Jim Burns / Natural Impacts
Page 81 © Gail Shumway
Page 82 © Erwin & Peggy Bauer
Page 83 © Barbara von Hoffmann
Page 85 © Jim Burns / Natural Impacts
Page 86 © garykramer.net
Page 87 © Jim Burns / Natural Impacts
Page 88 © Jim Burns / Natural Impacts
Page 90-91 © François Gohier / Ardea.com
Page 92 © Sanford/Agliolo / AlaskaStock.com
Page 93 © Cathy & Gordon ILLG
Page 94 © Jim Burns / Natural Impacts
Page 95 © Cathy & Gordon ILLG
Page 96 © Jim Burns / Natural Impacts
Page 98 © Jim Burns / Natural Impacts
Page 99 © Brian E. Small
Page 100 © Brian E. Small
Page 103 © Brian E. Small
Page 104 © Jim Burns / Natural Impacts
Page 105 © Jim Burns / Natural Impacts
Page 106 © Brian E. Small
Page 107 © Jim Burns / Natural Impacts
Page 108 © Art Wolfe
Page 109 © Anita Weiner
Page 110 © Richard Hamilton Smith
Page 113 © McCloskey / Peter Arnold, Inc.
Page 114 Left © Jim Burns / Natural Impacts
Page 114 Right © Gary R. Zahm
Page 115 © Michael H. Francis
Page 116 © Lynn M. Stone
Page 118 © Jim Burns / Natural Impacts
Page 119 © Brian E. Small
Page 120 © Lisa & Mike Husar / TeamHusar.com
Page 122-123 © Robert McCaw
Page 124 © Gail Shumway
Page 125 © Wendy Shattil / Bob Rozinski
Page 126 Top © Donald M. Jones
Page 126 Bottom © Lisa & Mike Husar / TeamHusar.com
Page 128 © Brian E. Small
Page 129 © Brian E. Small

CD Track contents

Track 1: Great Horned Owl

Track 2: Barred Owl

Track 3: Short-eared Owl

Track 4: Snowy Owl

Track 5: Spotted Owl

Track 6: Eastern Screech-Owl

Track 7: Western Screech-Owl

Track 8: Barn Owl

Track 9: Elf Owl

Track 10: Northern Saw-whet Owl

Track 11: Burrowing Owl

Track 12: Whiskered Screech-Owl

Track 13: Long-eared Owl

Track 14: Northern Pygmy-Owl

Track 15: Northern Hawk Owl

Track 16: Flammulated Owl

Track 17: Ferruginous Pygmy-Owl

Track 18: Boreal Owl

Track 19: Great Gray Owl